Neuroleadership

The Science Behind Exceptional Business
Leadership

Thomas Allan

KFT
PUBLISHING

KFT Publishing

Paperback ISBN: 978-0-6457786-8-7
Hardcover ISBN: 979-8-8702307-7-1

KFT

PUBLISHING

Contents

Foreword

I n an era where the landscape of business is perpetually evolving, the quest for effective leadership remains a constant pursuit. The emergence of neuroleadership as a field of study is not just a testament to this quest but also a revolutionary step towards redefining leadership itself. My journey towards writing this book, "Neuroleadership: Harnessing Brain Science for Effective Leadership," began with a simple yet profound realization: to lead others effectively, one must first understand the intricate workings of the human mind.

As a seasoned leader in the business world, I have witnessed firsthand the challenges and complexities that come with the role. From making critical decisions under pressure to motivating a diverse team, the demands of leadership are many and varied. However, traditional leadership models, while valuable, often fell short in addressing these challenges comprehensively. This gap led me to explore the burgeoning field of neuroleadership, where the mysteries of the brain meet the art of leadership.

This book is the culmination of extensive research and practical experience, aimed at providing leaders with a deeper understanding of how neuroscience can enhance their leadership abilities. It is designed to be a guide, a companion, and a source of inspiration for those who aspire to lead with more than just intuition and experience – those who seek to lead with an understanding of the brain's potential.

Readers can expect to embark on a journey through the various facets of neuroleadership. From the neuroscience of decision-making and emotional intelligence to the application of neuroethical principles in business, each chapter is crafted to provide valuable insights into how the brain influences leadership behaviors and strategies. The book is not just about theories and concepts; it is replete with practical applications, real-world examples, and strategies that can be implemented in daily leadership practices.

One of the core messages of this book is that leadership is not a static skill set but a dynamic process of continuous learning and adaptation. The brain's remarkable ability for neuroplasticity means that we can develop and enhance our leadership capabilities at any stage of our careers. This book aims to empower leaders to harness their brain's potential, cultivate a magnetic mindset, and lead their teams to new heights of success.

As you delve into the pages of this book, I invite you to keep an open mind and a willingness to explore new perspectives. Whether you are a seasoned executive, an aspiring leader, or simply someone fascinated by the intersection of neuroscience and leadership, this book has something for you. My hope is that it will not only enrich your understanding of leadership but also inspire you to apply these insights in a way that transforms your approach to leading others.

In closing, I leave you with a thought that has guided me throughout my journey in writing this book: "Leadership is an art that can be refined and perfected with the brush of neuroscience." Let this book be your palette as you paint your unique path in the world of leadership.

Sincerely,

Thomas Allan

Chapter One

Introduction to Neuroleadership

"The brain is the organ of destiny. It holds within its humming mechanism secrets that will determine the future of the human race." – Wilder Penfield

1. The Evolution of Leadership Studies

The study of leadership, a concept as old as civilization itself, has undergone significant transformations, reflecting the changing dynamics of society and organizations. This evolution is not just an academic journey but a reflection of our deepening understanding of what it means to lead effectively in diverse contexts.

Early Perspectives: The Trait-Based Approach

In the early stages, leadership studies were heavily influenced by the "Great Man" theory, which emerged in the 19th century. This theory, championed by historians like Thomas Carlyle, suggested that leaders were extraordinary individuals, born with innate qualities that predestined them for leadership. Key traits such as intelligence, charisma, decisiveness, and moral fortitude were considered essential markers of a natural-born leader. This perspective was appealing because it provided a simple explanation for complex leadership phenomena and celebrated the role of influential individuals in shaping history.

However, as the industrial age advanced and organizations became more complex, the limitations of the trait-based approach became apparent. It failed to account for the success of leaders who lacked these so-called inherent qualities. Moreover, it did not explain why some individuals who possessed these traits were unsuccessful leaders. This led to a growing recognition that leadership might be more nuanced than previously thought.

The Shift to Situational and Behavioral Models

The mid to late 20th century marked a significant shift in leadership studies, moving away from the trait-centric view. The emergence of situational and behavioral theories brought a new understanding of leadership as a dynamic and adaptable process. Kurt Lewin, often regarded as the father of social psychology, played a pivotal role in this transition. His research demonstrated that leadership effectiveness was not solely dependent on inherent traits but also on the behavior of leaders and their interaction with the environment.

Fred Fiedler's Contingency Model further advanced this idea by proposing that the effectiveness of a leader is contingent on both their leadership style and the favorableness of the leadership situation. This model was groundbreaking as it suggested that there was no one-size-fits-all approach to leadership. Instead, it highlighted the importance of adaptability and the need for leaders to modify their style to suit different situations and team dynamics.

Implications for Modern Leadership

The evolution from trait-based to situational and behavioral leadership models has profound implications for contemporary leadership development. It democratizes leadership, suggesting that effective leadership skills can be developed and are not the exclusive domain of a few 'naturally born' leaders. This shift has encouraged a more inclusive approach to leadership development, focusing on training, context-specific strategies, and behavioral flexibility.

Moreover, this evolution laid the groundwork for the emergence of neuroleadership. By acknowledging that effective leadership is influenced by a multitude of factors, including situational dynamics and learned behaviors, the field became ripe for integrating insights from neuroscience to further understand and enhance leadership effectiveness.

The journey of leadership studies from trait-based to situational and behavioral models represents a significant advancement in our understanding of what makes a leader effective. This evolution not only reflects changes in our societal and organizational structures but also paves the way for more scientific and inclusive approaches to leadership, such as neuroleadership.

2. Defining Neuroleadership

The advent of neuroleadership in the early 21st century marked a significant milestone in the evolution of leadership studies. This interdisciplinary field, at the confluence of neuroscience and leadership, offers a radical rethinking of leadership effectiveness through the prism of brain science. It represents a shift from purely psychological and behavioral models to a deeper, biologically-informed understanding of leadership.

The Convergence of Neuroscience and Leadership

Neuroleadership integrates the latest findings from neuroscience to shed light on how various brain processes influence key aspects of leadership. This includes understanding how leaders make decisions, regulate emotions, manage stress, and foster social connections within their teams. The premise is that by understanding the neurological basis of these processes, leadership can be more effectively taught, learned, and practiced.

Core Areas of Focus in Neuroleadership

1. **Decision-Making:** One of the central tenets of neuroleadership is understanding the neural mechanisms behind decision-making. Research in this area explores how the brain assesses risks, processes information, and balances emotional and rational inputs to make decisions. This knowledge is crucial for leaders who must often make complex decisions under pressure.

2. **Emotional Intelligence:** Emotional intelligence, a concept popularized by psychologist Daniel Goleman, is another key focus of neuroleadership. It involves understanding and managing one's own emotions and empathizing with others. Neuroleadership explores the neural bases of empathy, self-regulation, and social awareness, providing insights into how leaders can develop these critical skills.

3. **Social Interactions:** Leadership invariably involves managing relationships and influencing people. Neuroleadership examines how brain chemistry and structure impact social interactions, including trust-building, conflict resolution, and collaboration. Understanding these aspects can help leaders create more cohesive and effective teams.

4. **Neuroplasticity and Learning:** Neuroplasticity, or the brain's ability to reorganize itself by forming new neural connections throughout life, is a fundamental concept in neuroleadership. It underscores the capacity for change and development in leadership abilities, challenging the notion that leadership skills are static or fixed.

Implications for Leadership Development

The implications of neuroleadership for leadership development are profound. It suggests that effective leadership is not just a matter of personality or experience but also of how well a leader understands and leverages brain functioning. Neuroleadership provides a science-based framework for developing leadership skills, offering strategies that are aligned with how the brain naturally works and learns.

In essence, neuroleadership demystifies many aspects of leadership, providing a more nuanced and scientifically grounded understanding of what makes leaders effective. It empowers current and aspiring leaders with knowledge and techniques that can enhance their ability to lead, adapt, and thrive in complex organizational environments.

3. The Importance of Neuroleadership in Business

In the contemporary business landscape, characterized by rapid change, complexity, and technological advancement, neuroleadership has emerged as a vital tool for addressing some of the most pressing challenges faced by leaders. This approach not only complements traditional leadership theories but also provides a deeper, science-based understanding of leadership effectiveness.

Enhancing Decision-Making

One of the most critical aspects of leadership is decision-making. Neuroleadership sheds light on the neural mechanisms involved in making decisions, offering insights into how leaders can overcome cognitive biases and make more balanced, informed choices. This is particularly crucial in a business environment where decisions often have significant consequences and must be made under pressure. Understanding the brain's decision-making processes, including how it evaluates risks and rewards, can lead to more strategic and effective decision-making in business settings.

Improving Emotional Intelligence

Emotional intelligence is a cornerstone of effective leadership. Neuroleadership provides a neurological perspective on emotional regulation and empathy, crucial for resonant leadership. By understanding the brain's emotional processing, leaders can better manage their own emotions and more effectively understand and respond to the emotions of others. This insight is invaluable in building strong relationships, managing teams, and navigating the interpersonal complexities of the workplace.

Fostering Innovation and Creativity

Innovation and creativity are key drivers of business success. Neuroleadership explores how the brain generates new ideas and solves problems, offering leaders strategies to create environments that foster creative thinking and innovation. This includes understanding the conditions under which the brain is most likely to generate novel ideas and how to encourage creative thinking among team members. In an era where innovation is a competitive advantage, applying neuroscientific insights to cultivate creativity can be a game-changer for businesses.

Navigating Change

Change management is a significant challenge for leaders in any organization. Neuroleadership provides tools and insights to better manage and lead through change by understanding how the brain responds to uncertainty and new challenges. This knowledge can help leaders develop strategies to reduce resistance to change, facilitate smoother transitions, and build a culture that is more adaptable and resilient to change.

Conclusion

The integration of neuroscience into leadership development represents a significant advancement in our understanding of what it takes to lead effectively in today's business world. Neuroleadership offers practical, science-based solutions to real-world business challenges, paving the way for the development of leaders who are more adaptable, emotionally intelligent, and capable of fostering innovation and managing change. As organizations continue to navigate an increasingly complex and dynamic business environment, the principles of neuroleadership will be invaluable in guiding successful and effective leadership practices.

Chapter Two

The Neuroscience of Leadership

"**L**eadership is the capacity to translate vision into reality."
– Warren Bennis

1. Understanding the Brain's Role in Leadership

In the dynamic and complex arena of modern business, the role of effective leadership is more critical than ever. Leaders are not only tasked with making pivotal decisions but also with inspiring and guiding their teams through challenges and changes. This necessitates a deep understanding of the brain's role in leadership, a concept at the heart of neuroleadership.

The Brain: The Command Center for Leadership

Neuroleadership posits that the brain is the epicenter of all leadership activities. It's where critical skills like decision-making, emotional regulation, empathy, strategic thinking, and problem-solving originate.

The brain's intricate network of neurons and neurotransmitters orchestrates a leader's responses to various situations, influencing their effectiveness and impact.

Emotional Regulation and Empathy

One of the key areas where the brain's role is evident is in emotional regulation and empathy. The ability to understand and manage one's own emotions, as well as to recognize and respond to the emotions of others, is crucial in leadership. This emotional intelligence is rooted in specific brain areas, such as the amygdala and prefrontal cortex, which work together to process emotional information and guide appropriate responses.

Cognitive Flexibility and Strategic Thinking

Leadership also demands cognitive flexibility – the ability to adapt thinking and behavior in response to changing environments. This flexibility is governed by the brain's executive functions, located primarily in the prefrontal cortex. These functions enable leaders to plan, focus attention, remember instructions, and juggle multiple tasks successfully.

Communication and Social Cognition

Effective leadership is also about communication and understanding the social dynamics within a team. The brain's social cognition network, which includes regions like the temporoparietal junction and posterior cingulate cortex, plays a vital role in understanding others' perspectives, intentions, and emotions. This understanding is crucial for effective communication and team management.

Stress Management and Decision-Making

Leaders often face high-pressure situations that can induce stress. The brain's response to stress, particularly the release of cortisol, can significantly impact decision-making processes. Chronic stress can impair the prefrontal cortex, leading to less effective decision-making. Understanding the neuroscience of stress enables leaders to employ strategies to manage stress and maintain clear, rational decision-making even under pressure.

Implications for Leadership Development

Understanding the brain's role in leadership has profound implications for leadership development. It suggests that leadership skills can be developed and enhanced through targeted strategies that align with brain functioning. For instance, training in mindfulness and emotional intelligence can strengthen the brain's ability to regulate emotions and empathize with others.

Moreover, this understanding underscores the importance of creating a work environment that supports brain health, including managing stress, encouraging rest, and promoting mental well-being. Such an environment not only enhances individual leadership capabilities but also contributes to the overall effectiveness and resilience of the team.

Conclusion

The exploration of the brain's role in leadership is a cornerstone of neuroleadership. By understanding how various brain functions underpin key leadership skills, leaders can adopt more effective strategies to enhance their leadership capabilities. This chapter lays the foundation for a deeper dive into specific brain structures and functions, neuroplasticity, and their implications for leadership, which will be explored in the subsequent sections.

2. Key Brain Structures and Functions

Exploring the intricate network of the brain is essential for grasping the concept of neuroleadership and utilizing brain science to enhance leadership effectiveness. This section provides an in-depth look at key brain structures and their functions, highlighting their relevance to leadership capabilities and decision-making processes.

Prefrontal Cortex: The Executive Command Center

The prefrontal cortex (PFC) is pivotal in leadership. It's responsible for executive functions such as planning, problem-solving, decision-making, and impulse control. Leaders with a robust PFC demonstrate enhanced abilities to think strategically, make sound decisions, and remain composed under pressure. This area of the brain is crucial for tasks that require abstract thinking, long-term planning, and the assessment of risks and rewards.

Amygdala: The Emotional Processor

The amygdala, often termed the emotional center of the brain, is integral to how we process and respond to emotions. It plays a key role in emotional regulation, fear response, and the evaluation of potential threats and rewards. For leaders, understanding the amygdala's function is vital in managing personal emotional responses and in recognizing and responding to the emotional states of team members. This awareness can lead to a more empathetic leadership style and a positive workplace atmosphere.

Hippocampus: The Memory and Learning Hub

The hippocampus is central to memory formation and learning. In leadership, a strong hippocampus aids in absorbing new information, adapting to changes, and making informed decisions based on past experiences and learned knowledge. This aspect of the brain is crucial for leaders who need to recall important information, learn from previous situations, and navigate complex, evolving business landscapes.

Basal Ganglia: The Habit and Routine Center

The basal ganglia play a significant role in habit formation, routine behaviors, and motor activities. This structure helps leaders develop and maintain effective work habits and routines. Understanding how the basal ganglia influence behavior can assist leaders in establishing productive habits and routines, both personally and within their teams, leading to more efficient and streamlined work processes.

Anterior Cingulate Cortex: The Conflict Resolution and Empathy Area

The anterior cingulate cortex (ACC) is involved in attention regulation, conflict resolution, and empathy. A well-developed ACC enhances a leader's ability to focus, manage conflicts effectively, and empathize with others. This brain area is particularly important in leadership for navigating interpersonal dynamics, understanding team members' perspectives, and fostering a collaborative work environment.

Harnessing Neuroleadership for Optimal Performance

By understanding these key brain structures and their functions, leaders can apply neuroleadership principles to optimize their own brain function and create a work environment conducive to innovation, collaboration, and peak performance. This knowledge empowers leaders to enhance their decision-making, emotional intelligence, memory, habit formation, and empathy, ultimately leading to more effective and impactful leadership.

In conclusion, a deep understanding of the brain's key structures and their functions is crucial for leaders seeking to leverage neuroleadership effectively. Recognizing the roles of the prefrontal cortex, amygdala, hippocampus, basal ganglia, and anterior cingulate cortex allows leaders to unlock their full potential and foster a workplace that exemplifies exceptional business leadership.

3. Neuroplasticity and its Implications for Leadership

In the dynamic realm of business, the ability of leaders to adapt and evolve is not just an asset but a necessity. Neuroplasticity, the brain's ability to reorganize itself by forming new neural connections, stands at the forefront of this adaptive capability. This concept has revolutionized our understanding of personal and professional growth, particularly in leadership development.

Neuroplasticity: The Brain's Adaptive Power

Neuroplasticity debunks the myth of a static brain, revealing that our cognitive architecture is malleable and responsive to our experiences and learning practices. This adaptability is a beacon of hope for continuous personal and professional growth, suggesting that leadership skills are not fixed but can be cultivated and refined over time.

Continuous Learning and Growth Mindset

For leaders, the implications of neuroplasticity are profound. It underscores the importance of a growth mindset, a belief in the potential for fundamental development of one's abilities and intelligence. Leaders who embrace continuous learning keep their brains agile and open to new strategies, ideas, and innovations. This could involve engaging in diverse learning activities, such as professional courses, reading, or interactive workshops, which stimulate the brain and foster new neural pathways.

Deliberate Practice and Skill Enhancement

Neuroplasticity also highlights the significance of deliberate practice in leadership development. By repeatedly practicing specific leadership skills, whether it's strategic thinking, empathetic communication, or decision-making, leaders can strengthen the neural circuits associated with these skills. This process of focused and sustained practice can lead to significant improvements in leadership competencies.

Creating a Supportive Growth Environment

Leadership is not just about personal development; it's also about cultivating an environment that encourages growth among team members. Neuroplasticity suggests that leaders have the responsibility to create a culture that values learning, experimentation, and feedback. This can be achieved by providing opportunities for team members to take on new challenges, offering constructive feedback, and recognizing their efforts and achievements. Such an environment not only nurtures individual growth but also contributes to the collective intelligence and adaptability of the organization.

Conclusion: Embracing Neuroplasticity for Leadership Excellence

Neuroplasticity offers a transformative perspective on leadership development. It empowers leaders to continuously refine their skills and adapt to the ever-changing business landscape. By embracing the principles of neuroplasticity, leaders can foster a culture of continuous learning and innovation, driving their organizations towards sustained success and resilience in a competitive world.

Chapter Three

Emotional Intelligence and Leadership

"Emotional intelligence does not mean merely 'being nice'. At strategic moments it may demand not 'being nice', but rather, for example, bluntly confronting someone with an uncomfortable but consequential truth they've been avoiding." – Daniel Goleman

1. The Role of Emotions in Leadership

In the realm of leadership, emotions play a pivotal role, often serving as a driving force behind decision-making, team dynamics, and organizational culture. Understanding the role of emotions in leadership is crucial for effective management and inspiring leadership.

Emotions as a Leadership Tool

Emotions are not just personal experiences; they are also powerful communicative tools. Leaders who understand and harness their emotional experiences can better connect with their team members, inspire confidence, and motivate action. Emotional expressions can convey empathy, enthusiasm, concern, or determination, influencing the emotional climate of the entire team or organization.

Emotional Contagion in Leadership

Leaders often set the emotional tone of their environment. This phenomenon, known as emotional contagion, suggests that the emotions displayed by leaders can be 'contagious' and significantly impact the mood and attitudes of their team members. A leader who consistently demonstrates positive emotions like optimism and resilience can foster a more positive work atmosphere, whereas a leader prone to negativity or stress can contribute to a tense or demotivating environment.

Decision-Making and Emotional Information

Emotions also play a critical role in decision-making processes. Contrary to the traditional view that emotions are hindrances to rational decision-making, recent research suggests that emotions can provide essential information and enhance decision-making capabilities. Leaders who are attuned to their emotions and those of others can make more nuanced and empathetic decisions.

Empathy and Relational Leadership

Empathy, a core component of emotional intelligence, is particularly important in leadership. It involves understanding and sharing the feelings of others. Empathetic leaders are better equipped to build strong relationships, resolve conflicts, and understand the needs and motivations of their team members. This understanding can lead to more effective team management and improved employee satisfaction and loyalty.

Embracing Emotional Leadership

In summary, the role of emotions in leadership is multifaceted and significant. Emotions are not only central to how leaders relate to their teams and make decisions but also play a key role in shaping the emotional and psychological climate of the workplace. Leaders who understand and effectively manage emotions can inspire, motivate, and lead their teams more effectively, contributing to the overall success and health of their organizations.

2. Developing Emotional Intelligence

Building on the understanding of the role of emotions in leadership, it becomes evident that developing emotional intelligence (EI) is a key step for leaders aiming to harness the power of emotions effectively. Emotional intelligence, the ability to recognize, understand, and manage our own emotions and those of others, is a skill that can be developed and refined over time.

Self-Awareness: The Foundation of EI

The journey to developing EI begins with self-awareness. This involves understanding one's own emotions, triggers, and responses. Leaders who are self-aware can recognize how their feelings affect their thoughts and behaviors and can adjust accordingly. Techniques such as mindfulness and reflective practices can enhance self-awareness.

Self-Regulation: Managing Emotions

Once aware of their emotional states, leaders must learn to manage and regulate these emotions. This doesn't mean suppressing emotions but rather understanding and channeling them in productive ways. Self-regulation is crucial in maintaining objectivity and making reasoned decisions, especially in high-pressure situations.

Empathy: Understanding Others

Developing empathy is another critical aspect of EI. This goes beyond simply recognizing the emotions of others; it involves genuinely understanding and sharing in these feelings. Empathetic leaders can build deeper connections with their team members, fostering trust and open communication. Techniques to enhance empathy include active listening and perspective-taking exercises.

Social Skills: Navigating Interpersonal Dynamics

Effective social skills are the outward manifestation of EI. This includes the ability to communicate effectively, resolve conflicts, and inspire and influence others. Leaders with strong social skills can navigate the complexities of interpersonal dynamics in the workplace, leading to more cohesive and productive teams.

Continuous Learning and Development

Developing EI is not a one-time effort but a continuous process. Leaders should seek ongoing opportunities for learning and growth, such as EI training programs, coaching, and feedback from peers and mentors. This commitment to continuous development is essential for leaders to remain effective and responsive in an ever-changing business environment.

The Path to Enhanced Leadership through EI

In conclusion, developing emotional intelligence is a transformative process for leaders. It starts with self-awareness and extends to managing one's own emotions, understanding and empathizing with others, and effectively navigating social interactions. By investing in the development of EI, leaders can enhance their ability to connect with, inspire, and lead their teams more effectively, ultimately contributing to the success and well-being of their organizations.

3. Applying Emotional Intelligence in Business

Having developed emotional intelligence (EI), the next crucial step for leaders is to apply these skills effectively in the business context. The application of EI in business can significantly enhance leadership effectiveness, team dynamics, and organizational performance.

Emotional Intelligence in Communication

Effective communication is a cornerstone of successful leadership, and EI plays a critical role in this. Leaders with high EI are adept at adjusting their communication style to suit the emotional states and needs of their audience. For instance, a leader might use more empathetic language and tone when addressing a team member going through a challenging time, thereby fostering a supportive and understanding work environment.

Example: A manager notices a team member appearing disengaged and learns through empathetic dialogue that the individual is facing personal challenges. By acknowledging these challenges and offering support, the manager not only helps the individual but also maintains team morale.

Conflict Resolution

Conflict is inevitable in any workplace, and how it's managed can either strengthen or weaken a team. Leaders with high EI can navigate conflicts by understanding the emotions involved and finding common ground. They can mediate discussions in a way that acknowledges each party's feelings and perspectives, leading to more amicable and effective resolutions.

Example: During a team disagreement on project direction, a leader with high EI recognizes the underlying concerns and emotions of each team member. By addressing these concerns and facilitating a collaborative discussion, the leader helps the team reach a consensus that respects everyone's viewpoints.

Motivating and Inspiring Teams

Leaders with high EI can inspire and motivate their teams effectively. They understand what drives their team members and can tailor their motivational strategies accordingly. This might involve recognizing individual achievements, understanding team members' career aspirations, or creating a positive and inclusive team culture.

Example: A leader uses individualized motivational techniques, such as offering professional development opportunities to those who value growth or public recognition for those who appreciate acknowledgment, thereby boosting overall team motivation and engagement.

Managing Change

Change management is another area where EI is invaluable. Leaders who are emotionally intelligent can better understand and address the concerns and anxieties that change can bring. They can communicate changes in a way that is sensitive to team members' emotions, helping to facilitate smoother transitions and maintain morale.

Example: When implementing a major organizational change, an emotionally intelligent leader holds open forums and one-on-one meetings to address employees' concerns, reducing resistance and fostering a sense of security and trust.

EI as a Business Imperative

In summary, applying emotional intelligence in business is not just beneficial; it's imperative for modern leadership. Whether it's through effective communication, conflict resolution, motivating teams, or managing change, EI enables leaders to navigate the complex emotional landscape of the workplace. By applying EI, leaders can create a more harmonious, productive, and resilient organization.

Chapter Four

Cognitive Processes and Decision Making

"The human brain had a vast memory storage. It made us curious and very creative. Those were the characteristics that gave us an advantage - curiosity, creativity, and memory. And that brain did something very special. It invented an idea called 'the future.'" – David Suzuki

1. The Science behind Decision Making

In the realm of leadership, decision-making is a critical skill. It's a complex process that involves both conscious reasoning and subconscious influences. Understanding the neuroscience behind decision-making can empower leaders to make more informed, effective choices.

Neural Foundations of Decision Making

Decision-making primarily involves the prefrontal cortex, the part of the brain responsible for higher-order cognitive processes such as planning, reasoning, and problem-solving. This area assesses available information, weighs risks and benefits, and helps form logical conclusions.

The Role of the Limbic System

The limbic system, particularly the amygdala, plays a crucial role in emotional processing. Emotions significantly influence decision-making, often serving as a shortcut to quick judgments. However, they can also lead to biased or irrational decisions if not properly managed.

Example: A leader might feel a strong emotional reaction (fear, excitement) to a risky business opportunity. While these emotions provide valuable information, relying solely on them can lead to impulsive decisions.

Dopamine and Reward-Based Decisions

Dopamine, a neurotransmitter associated with pleasure and reward, influences decision-making. It affects how leaders assess the potential rewards of a decision and can drive risk-taking behavior. Understanding this can help leaders balance the pursuit of rewarding outcomes with rational risk assessment.

Neuroscience and Rational Decision Making

While emotions and rewards play a role, effective decision-making also requires rational analysis. The integration of emotional and rational processes in the brain is key to balanced decision-making. Leaders who understand this can better navigate complex decisions, balancing gut feelings with logical analysis.

The Impact of Stress on Decision Making

Stress can significantly impair decision-making abilities. Under stress, the brain's focus narrows, often leading to short-term, survival-oriented thinking. This can be counterproductive in a business context, where long-term, strategic thinking is essential.

Strategies for Improved Decision Making

1. Mindfulness and Reflection:

- **Daily Mindfulness Practice:** Leaders can set aside time each day for mindfulness exercises like meditation or deep breathing. This practice helps in calming the mind, increasing focus, and reducing the impact of stress on decision-making.

- **Reflective Journaling:** Keeping a journal to reflect on daily decisions can help leaders understand their thought processes and identify patterns or biases in their decision-making.

2. Diverse Perspectives:

- **Establishing a Decision-Making Panel:** Create a diverse group of individuals from different departments or backgrounds to provide input on major decisions. This can help in gaining a variety of perspectives and mitigating personal biases.

- **Encouraging Constructive Dissent:** Foster an organizational culture where team members feel comfortable voicing differing opinions. This can challenge leaders to consider alternative viewpoints and make more informed decisions.

3. Structured Decision-Making Processes:

- **SWOT Analysis:** Before making a decision, conduct a SWOT analysis (Strengths, Weaknesses, Opportunities, Threats) to systematically evaluate all aspects of a situation.

- **Decision Trees:** Use decision trees to map out the possible outcomes of different choices. This visual tool can help in understanding the potential impact of each decision.

4. Scenario Planning:

- **Future Scenario Exercises:** Regularly engage in exercises that envision various future scenarios. This helps in preparing for different possibilities and making decisions that are robust under various future conditions.

5. Continuous Learning:

- **Case Studies:** Analyze case studies relevant to your industry to understand how other leaders have navigated similar decisions. This can provide valuable insights and lessons.

- **Professional Development:** Attend workshops, seminars, or courses focused on decision-making and critical thinking skills.

6. Leveraging Technology:

- **Data Analytics Tools:** Utilize data analytics tools to gather and analyze data that can inform decisions. This helps in making decisions based on empirical evidence rather than intuition alone.

- **Simulation Software:** Use simulation software to model the outcomes of different decision paths. This can provide a risk-free environment to explore the consequences of various choices.

7. Time Management:

- **Avoiding Rushed Decisions:** Allocate sufficient time for important decisions. Rushed decisions are more prone to errors and biases.

- **Setting Decision Deadlines:** While avoiding haste, it's also important to set deadlines to ensure decisions are made in a timely manner.

8. Emotional Regulation:

- **Recognizing Emotional States:** Be aware of how your current emotional state may influence your decision-making. If necessary, delay important decisions until you can approach them with a clear mind.

- **Seeking Feedback on Emotional Intelligence:** Regularly seek feedback from trusted colleagues or mentors on how well you manage your emotions in decision-making contexts.

By incorporating these strategies, leaders can significantly improve their decision-making processes, leading to more effective and successful leadership outcomes.

Conclusion

Understanding the neuroscience behind decision-making is vital for leaders. It provides insights into how to balance emotional and rational thinking, manage the influence of stress, and make decisions that are both informed and intuitive. By applying these insights, leaders can enhance their decision-making skills, leading to better outcomes for their organizations.

However, Artificial Intelligence (AI) is increasingly playing a pivotal role in decision-making processes across various sectors. As AI technology advances, its impact on decision-making is becoming more profound and multifaceted. Here are key areas where AI is influencing decision-making:

1. Data Analysis and Insights:

- **Enhanced Data Processing:** AI can analyze vast amounts of data much faster and more accurately than humans. This capability allows for the extraction of meaningful insights from big data, which can inform decision-making.

- **Predictive Analytics:** AI algorithms can identify patterns and trends in data, enabling predictive analytics. This helps leaders make decisions based on future projections, improving strategic planning and risk management.

2. Automating Routine Decisions:

- **Operational Efficiency:** AI can automate routine and repetitive decision-making processes, such as scheduling, inventory management, and basic customer service inquiries. This automation increases operational efficiency and allows human decision-makers to focus on more complex strategic decisions.

3. Enhancing Decision Accuracy:

- **Reducing Human Bias:** AI systems, when properly designed, can help reduce human biases in decision-making by providing data-driven recommendations.

- **Consistency in Decisions:** AI ensures consistency in

decision-making, especially in areas where uniformity and adherence to rules are important.

4. Decision Support Systems:

- **Real-Time Assistance:** AI-powered decision support systems can provide real-time information and recommendations, aiding leaders in making informed decisions quickly.

- **Scenario Analysis:** AI can simulate various scenarios based on different decision paths, helping leaders understand potential outcomes and implications.

5. Personalized Experiences:

- **Customer Engagement:** In marketing and customer service, AI can analyze customer data to personalize interactions and improve customer engagement strategies.

- **Tailored Recommendations:** AI systems can provide personalized recommendations to customers, enhancing user experience and decision-making in purchasing.

6. Ethical and Governance Implications:

- **Ethical Decision-Making:** As AI becomes more involved in decision-making, there's a growing need to address ethical considerations, such as fairness, transparency, and accountability.

- **Regulatory Compliance:** AI can assist in ensuring decisions comply with legal and regulatory standards, reducing the risk of non-compliance.

7. Future Trends and Developments:

- **Advancements in AI:** Ongoing advancements in AI, such as improvements in natural language processing and machine learning, will continue to refine decision-making tools.

- **Integration with Other Technologies:** The integration of AI with other emerging technologies like the Internet of Things (IoT) and blockchain could lead to new decision-making capabilities.

AI's role in decision-making is transformative, offering enhanced data analysis, automation of routine tasks, decision support, and personalized experiences. However, it's crucial to approach AI integration thoughtfully, considering ethical implications and ensuring that AI complements human judgment rather than replacing it. As AI technology evolves, it will continue to reshape how decisions are made in business and beyond.

2. Cognitive Biases and their Impact on Leadership

Cognitive biases, the systematic patterns of deviation from norm or rationality in judgment, play a significant role in leadership. These biases can affect decision-making processes, interpersonal relations, and strategic planning. Understanding and mitigating the impact of these biases is crucial for effective leadership.

Types of Cognitive Biases Affecting Leadership:

1. Confirmation Bias: The tendency to search for, interpret, favor, and recall information in a way that confirms one's preexisting beliefs or hypotheses. Leaders might ignore contrary information, leading to poor decision-making.

2. Overconfidence Bias: This occurs when a leader overestimates their own abilities or the accuracy of their information. It can lead to taking unnecessary risks or failing to seek additional information.

3. Anchoring Bias: The tendency to rely too heavily on the first piece of information encountered (the "anchor") when making decisions. Leaders might base their decisions on initial information without considering subsequent data.

4. Status Quo Bias: The preference for the current state of affairs. This bias can prevent leaders from embracing necessary changes or innovative ideas.

5. Groupthink: Occurs when a group values harmony and coherence over accurate analysis and critical evaluation. It can lead to poor decision-making and a lack of creativity in teams.

6. Self-Serving Bias: The tendency to attribute successes to internal factors while attributing failures to external factors. This can hinder a leader's ability to learn from mistakes.

Impact on Leadership:

- Impaired Decision-Making: Biases can lead to flawed judgments and decisions that are not based on objective analysis.

- Reduced Innovation: Cognitive biases can stifle creativity and innovation, as leaders may not explore all possible solutions to a problem.

- Ineffective Communication: Biases can affect how leaders communicate with and perceive feedback from their teams, potentially leading to misunderstandings and conflict.

- Poor Risk Management: Overconfidence and other biases can result in underestimating risks, leading to decisions that jeopardize the organization.

- Team Dynamics: Biases like groupthink can negatively impact team dynamics, reducing diversity of thought and critical analysis.

Strategies to Mitigate Cognitive Biases:

1. Awareness and Education: Regular training and awareness programs can help leaders recognize and understand their own cognitive biases.

2. Diverse Teams: Encouraging diversity in teams can provide a range of perspectives, helping to counteract individual biases.

3. Structured Decision-Making Processes: Implementing structured processes for decision-making can reduce the influence of individual biases.

4. Seeking External Input: Consulting with external advisors or stakeholders can provide an objective viewpoint, countering internal biases.

5. Reflection and Feedback: Encouraging a culture of feedback and self-reflection can help leaders identify and address their biases.

6. Debiasing Techniques: Techniques like considering the opposite, pre-mortem analysis (anticipating what could go wrong), and scenario planning can help in reducing biases.

In conclusion, cognitive biases can significantly impact leadership effectiveness. By recognizing and actively working to mitigate these biases, leaders can make more rational decisions, foster innovation, and lead their teams more effectively.

3. Improving Decision Making through Neuroscience Insights

The field of neuroscience offers valuable insights into how the brain makes decisions, providing leaders with strategies to enhance their decision-making processes. Understanding the neural mechanisms behind decision-making can lead to more rational, effective, and innovative leadership.

Neuroscientific Foundations of Decision Making:

1. Neural Basis of Decision Making: Decision-making involves various brain regions, primarily the prefrontal cortex, which is responsible for executive functions like planning, reasoning, and problem-solving. Understanding how this area functions can help leaders in making more considered decisions.

2. Emotion and Rationality: The amygdala, a region associated with emotional processing, also plays a crucial role in decision-making. Neuroscience shows that emotions and rational thinking are interconnected, challenging the traditional dichotomy between emotion and logic in decision-making.

3. Stress and Decision Making: Under stress, the brain's ability to make well-reasoned decisions can be impaired. The release of stress hormones like cortisol can affect the functioning of the prefrontal cortex, leading to more impulsive decisions.

Strategies for Improved Decision Making:

1. Mindfulness and Reflection: Mindfulness practices can enhance the functioning of the prefrontal cortex, leading to better

decision-making. Regular reflection allows leaders to be more aware of their thought processes and biases.

2. Emotional Regulation: Understanding the role of emotions in decision-making can help leaders manage their emotions more effectively. Techniques like emotional reappraisal or mindfulness can aid in better emotional regulation.

3. Stress Management: Implementing stress reduction techniques such as deep breathing, exercise, or meditation can improve decision-making abilities by reducing the negative impact of stress on the brain.

4. Cognitive Flexibility: Encouraging cognitive flexibility, the ability to adapt thinking in response to changing goals or environments, is crucial. This can be enhanced through activities that challenge the brain, such as learning new skills or engaging in complex problem-solving.

5. Sleep and Decision Making: Adequate sleep is essential for the brain's health and its decision-making capabilities. Leaders should prioritize sleep to maintain cognitive functions like memory, attention, and problem-solving.

6. Collaborative Decision Making: Engaging diverse teams in the decision-making process can counteract individual biases and lead to more comprehensive and effective decisions.

7. Neurofeedback and Training: Advanced techniques like neurofeedback can help leaders understand their brain activity patterns and train their brains for better decision-making.

Examples and Case Studies:

- Mindfulness in Leadership: Google's "Search Inside Yourself" program, which focuses on mindfulness and emotional intelligence, has been shown to improve decision-making and leadership effectiveness.

- Neurofeedback for Executives: Executives using neurofeedback have reported improvements in focus, stress management, and decision-making abilities.

- Sleep Research: Studies have shown that lack of sleep can significantly impair judgment and decision-making skills. Companies like Procter & Gamble and Goldman Sachs have implemented sleep hygiene training for their employees.

Neuroscience provides a wealth of insights that can significantly improve leadership decision-making. By understanding and applying these neuroscientific principles, leaders can enhance their cognitive and emotional skills, leading to more effective and informed decisions in their professional and personal lives.

Chapter Five

Motivation and Reward Systems

"**P**eople often say that motivation doesn't last. Well, neither does bathing – that's why we recommend it daily." – Zig Ziglar

1. The Neurobiology of Motivation

Understanding the neurobiology of motivation is crucial for leaders aiming to inspire and drive their teams effectively. Motivation, at its core, is a complex neurological process involving several key brain areas and neurotransmitter systems. This understanding can help leaders develop strategies to enhance motivation within their organizations.

Key Brain Structures in Motivation:

1. Mesolimbic Dopamine System: Often referred to as the brain's reward pathway, this system plays a central role in motivation. The release of dopamine in areas like the nucleus accumbens is associated with the anticipation of reward and is crucial for

goal-directed behavior.

2. Prefrontal Cortex: This region is involved in planning complex cognitive behavior and decision-making. It helps in setting goals and anticipating outcomes, which are key aspects of motivation.

3. Amygdala: Known for its role in processing emotions, the amygdala also influences motivation, particularly in response to emotionally charged stimuli or rewards.

4. Hippocampus: While primarily associated with memory, the hippocampus also plays a role in motivation by linking past experiences with future goals and rewards.

Neurotransmitters and Motivation:

1. Dopamine: Often labeled as the "feel-good" neurotransmitter, dopamine is crucial for pleasure and reward-seeking behavior. Its release can enhance motivation, particularly towards activities that are perceived as rewarding.

2. Serotonin: This neurotransmitter is associated with mood regulation. Higher levels of serotonin can lead to increased motivation and a more positive outlook, which is conducive to goal pursuit.

3. Norepinephrine: Involved in the body's stress response, norepinephrine can affect motivation by increasing arousal and alertness, thus enhancing focus and energy towards tasks.

Implications for Leadership:

- Understanding Individual Differences: Recognizing that motivation varies among individuals, partly due to neurological differences, can help leaders tailor their motivational strategies.

- Goal Setting: Effective goal setting, aligned with the individual's values and interests, can stimulate the brain's reward system, enhancing motivation.

- Feedback and Recognition: Positive feedback can trigger dopamine release, reinforcing motivation. Regular, meaningful recognition can therefore be a powerful motivator.

- Creating a Positive Environment: A work environment that promotes a positive mood can boost serotonin levels, thereby enhancing motivation and productivity.

- Challenging Yet Achievable Tasks: Assigning tasks that are challenging but achievable can stimulate the reward system, increasing motivation and engagement.

Real-World Applications:

Gamification in the Workplace: Implementing game-like elements in work tasks can activate the reward system, making mundane tasks more engaging and motivating.

Example: Sales Performance: A tech company implemented a gamified system for its sales team, where employees earned points for meeting certain targets, which could be exchanged for rewards. This approach tapped into the dopamine-driven reward system, making the sales process more engaging and motivating.

Learning and Development: An e-learning platform used gamification elements like badges, leaderboards, and progress tracking to motivate employees to complete training modules. This approach made learning more interactive and rewarding, leading to higher completion rates and better engagement.

Personalized Incentives: Understanding what rewards are most meaningful to each team member can make motivational strategies more effective.

Customized Rewards Program: A marketing firm introduced a personalized rewards system where employees could choose their incentives from a range of options, including extra vacation days, gym memberships, or tickets to events. This strategy recognized individual differences in what employees find motivating, leading to increased job satisfaction and performance.

Employee Recognition Platform: A multinational corporation used a digital platform where employees could give and receive recognition in the form of 'kudos' or points, which could be redeemed for various rewards. This system allowed for immediate and personalized recognition, enhancing the sense of achievement and motivation.

Stress Management Programs: Since excessive stress can impair the motivational pathways, offering stress management resources can help maintain high levels of motivation.

Mindfulness and Relaxation Workshops: A financial services company offered regular mindfulness and stress management workshops. These sessions helped employees manage stress, thereby preventing burnout and maintaining motivation levels.

Flexible Working Arrangements: To reduce stress and improve work-life balance, a software company introduced flexible working hours and the option to work from home. This policy acknowledged the impact of stress on motivation and productivity, leading to more motivated and engaged employees.

Creating a Positive Work Environment:

Office Design for Well-being: An architecture firm redesigned its office space to include more natural light, green areas, and relaxation zones. This environment aimed to boost serotonin levels, thereby enhancing mood and motivation among employees.

Team-Building Retreats: An organization organized annual team-building retreats which included outdoor activities and workshops. These retreats helped in building stronger team relationships and a more positive work culture, contributing to overall motivation.

Challenge and Skill Development:

Professional Growth Opportunities: A retail company offered a 'rising star' program that provided high-potential employees with challenging projects and skill development opportunities. This approach tapped into the employees' desire for growth and learning, keeping them motivated and engaged.

Mentorship Programs: A healthcare organization implemented a mentorship program where experienced professionals mentored younger employees. This program provided both mentors and mentees with new challenges and learning opportunities, fostering motivation through personal and professional development.

These examples illustrate how understanding the neurobiology of motivation can be practically applied in various business settings to enhance employee motivation, engagement, and productivity.

The neurobiology of motivation provides valuable insights for leaders. By understanding and leveraging the brain's motivation systems, leaders can create strategies that effectively motivate their teams, leading to enhanced performance and job satisfaction.

2. Understanding Intrinsic and Extrinsic Motivation

In the realm of leadership and organizational management, understanding the nuances of intrinsic and extrinsic motivation is pivotal for fostering a motivated workforce. These two types of motivation, though different in their sources, play a crucial role in driving employee behavior and performance.

Intrinsic Motivation:

- Definition: Intrinsic motivation arises from within the individual. It is driven by personal interest, enjoyment, or a sense of fulfillment derived from the task itself.

- Neurological Basis: Activities that are intrinsically motivating are often linked to the release of dopamine in the brain, associated with pleasure and reward. When employees engage in tasks they find genuinely interesting, this neurochemical response enhances their focus, creativity, and persistence.

- Examples in Business:

  - Autonomy: Allowing employees to have a say in how they complete their tasks can increase intrinsic motivation. For instance, a software company giving its developers the freedom to choose their coding methods or project approaches can lead to more innovative solutions.

  - Mastery and Skill Development: Opportunities for professional growth and skill enhancement, such as training programs or challenging assignments, can intrinsically motivate employees by fulfilling their desire for personal achievement and competence.

Extrinsic Motivation:

- Definition: Extrinsic motivation is driven by external factors, such as rewards, recognition, or avoiding negative outcomes.

- Neurological Basis: This form of motivation often involves the brain's reward system but is more closely tied to the anticipation of external rewards or the avoidance of negative consequences, rather than the pleasure of the activity itself.

- Examples in Business:

  - Performance Bonuses: Financial incentives for meeting or exceeding targets can be a powerful extrinsic motivator. For example, a sales team receiving bonuses for achieving their quarterly sales goals.

  - Recognition Programs: Public recognition, awards, or even simple acknowledgments in team meetings can serve as extrinsic motivators. An employee of the month award is a classic example of this.

Balancing Intrinsic and Extrinsic Motivation:

- Leadership Challenge: The challenge for leaders lies in striking the right balance between intrinsic and extrinsic motivators. Over-reliance on extrinsic rewards can sometimes undermine intrinsic motivation, especially if the rewards become the sole focus.

- Cultivating a Motivating Environment: Creating an environment that values both types of motivation involves recognizing individual differences in what motivates employees, providing a mix of intrinsic and extrinsic motivators, and aligning them with organizational goals.

- Example of Balanced Approach: A tech company might offer a mix of professional development opportunities (intrinsic) and performance-based bonuses (extrinsic) to motivate its engineers. This approach caters to both the engineers' desire for personal growth and their need for tangible rewards.

In summary, understanding and effectively leveraging both intrinsic and extrinsic motivation are key to fostering a motivated and productive workforce. Leaders who skillfully integrate these motivational strategies can enhance employee engagement, satisfaction, and organizational performance.

3. Creating a Rewarding Work Environment

Creating a rewarding work environment is a multifaceted endeavor that requires leaders to understand and effectively respond to the diverse needs and motivations of their team members. In "Magnetic Culture," a concept explored in my book "The Magnetic Mindset: Unlocking the Secrets of Influence and Persuasion," the emphasis is on leading by example, fostering a vibrant work culture, and mastering the art of rewards and recognition.

Lead by Example:

- Personal Influence: Leaders set the tone for the organizational culture. Their behavior, attitudes, and values are contagious and can significantly influence the work environment.

- Authenticity and Trust: By being authentic and trustworthy, leaders can create a strong emotional connection with their team, which is essential for a magnetic culture.

Fostering a Vibrant Work Culture:

- Positive Environment: A vibrant work culture is characterized by positivity, open communication, and mutual respect. It's about creating a space where employees feel valued and empowered.

- Inclusivity and Collaboration: Encouraging inclusivity and collaboration not only enhances team dynamics but also contributes to a more innovative and productive work environment.

Key to Rewards and Recognition:

- Understanding Individual Needs: Effective rewards and recognition go beyond one-size-fits-all approaches. It involves understanding what motivates each team member, whether it's public recognition, financial incentives, or opportunities for professional growth.

- Regular and Meaningful Recognition: Recognition should be regular and meaningful. It could range from acknowledging an employee's effort in a team meeting to more formal awards or promotions.

Transforming Mindset for Influence:

- Influence through Empathy: I emphasizes the importance of empathy in leadership. Understanding and relating to employees' perspectives can significantly enhance a leader's influence.

- Shaping Destiny through Leadership: Leaders have the power to shape the destiny of their organizations. By creating a magnetic culture, they can attract and retain top talent, drive innovation, and achieve sustainable success.

Practical Strategies:

- Mentorship Programs: Implementing mentorship programs where experienced employees guide newcomers can foster a sense of belonging and accelerate professional development.

  - Structured Mentor-Mentee Pairings: A tech company might implement a program where senior developers are paired with junior developers. The pairs meet regularly to discuss career goals, technical skills, and professional challenges. This not only accelerates the learning curve for junior staff but also provides leadership development opportunities for senior team members.

  - Cross-Departmental Mentoring: A multinational corporation could establish a cross-departmental mentorship program, allowing employees from different areas (like marketing and finance) to learn from each other. This approach broadens understanding across the organization and fosters interdepartmental collaboration.

  - Reverse Mentoring: In a reverse mentoring setup, younger or less experienced employees mentor senior staff about areas such as digital technology, social media, or current market trends. This can be particularly effective in organizations undergoing digital transformation.

- Flexible Work Arrangements: Offering flexible work arrangements can show that the organization values work-life balance, leading to increased job satisfaction and loyalty.

  - Telecommuting Options: A consulting firm might offer employees the option to work from home two days a week. This flexibility can help employees manage their personal commitments more effectively, leading to increased job satisfaction and productivity.

  - Flexible Hours: A retail business could allow store managers to set their own schedules, within certain limits, to accommodate peak times and personal responsibilities. This flexibility acknowledges the varying demands of the job and the individual's needs.

  - Compressed Workweeks: An option for a compressed workweek, where employees work longer hours for four days and take the fifth day off, can be offered by a manufacturing company. This arrangement can improve work-life balance and reduce commuting stress.

- Celebrating Milestones: Regularly celebrating both individual and team milestones can boost morale and reinforce a sense of accomplishment.

  - **Employee Anniversary Celebrations:** An IT company might celebrate employee work anniversaries with a special mention in the company newsletter and a small gift or bonus. Recognizing tenure shows appreciation for the employee's long-term commitment.

  - **Project Completion Parties:** After the successful completion of a major project, a construction firm could host a celebration event for the team. This not only acknowledges the hard work and success of the project but also boosts team morale.

- ○ **Personal Achievement Acknowledgment:** A law firm could acknowledge personal milestones of its staff, such as completing a degree or certification, with a congratulatory note from the leadership and a mention in team meetings. This shows the firm's support for personal as well as professional growth.

Implementing these strategies can significantly contribute to creating a rewarding work environment, where employees feel valued, supported, and motivated to achieve their best.

Creating a rewarding work environment is about much more than just financial incentives. It's about cultivating a magnetic culture where employees feel genuinely connected, valued, and motivated to contribute their best. As I have illustrated in "The Magnetic Mindset," the key lies in transforming leadership approaches to become more empathetic, influential, and visionary, thereby shaping a positive and productive organizational destiny.

Chapter Six

Social Neuroscience and Leadership

"None of us is as smart as all of us." – Ken Blanchard

1. The Importance of Social Connections in Leadership

In the realm of leadership, the significance of social connections cannot be overstated. The ability to forge and maintain strong relationships is not just a desirable trait but a fundamental aspect of effective leadership. This chapter delves into the importance of social connections in leadership, drawing on insights from social neuroscience.

Social Neuroscience Perspective:

- Human Brain as a Social Organ: Social neuroscience reveals that the human brain is inherently social. Our brains are wired to connect with others, and these connections significantly impact our thoughts, emotions, and behaviors.

- Mirror Neurons and Empathy: The discovery of mirror neurons has provided a neurological basis for empathy in leadership. These neurons enable us to understand and resonate with others' emotions, an essential skill for building strong relationships.

Impact on Leadership:

- Enhanced Team Dynamics: Leaders who prioritize social connections tend to foster more cohesive and collaborative teams. Strong social bonds within a team can lead to improved communication, trust, and collective problem-solving.

- Increased Employee Engagement: When leaders connect with their team members on a personal level, it can significantly boost morale and engagement. Employees who feel understood and valued by their leaders are more likely to be committed and motivated.

Developing Social Connections:

- Active Listening: Effective leaders practice active listening, showing genuine interest in their team members' thoughts and concerns. This not only helps in gathering valuable insights but also strengthens interpersonal relationships.

- Regular Check-ins: Scheduling regular one-on-one meetings with team members can help leaders stay connected with their individual needs and aspirations, fostering a sense of belonging and loyalty.

Challenges and Solutions:

- Overcoming Virtual Barriers: In a world increasingly reliant on virtual communication, maintaining social connections can be challenging. Leaders need to be creative in using technology to sustain engagement, such as through virtual team-building activities or regular video check-ins.

- Cultural Sensitivity: Leaders must also be aware of and sensitive to cultural differences in social interactions. Understanding diverse communication The importance of social connections in leadership is a critical aspect that goes beyond mere networking. It's about creating meaningful relationships that enhance team performance, employee satisfaction, and overall organizational success. Leaders who understand and apply the principles of social neuroscience in this context can significantly enhance their effectiveness and influence.

2. Building Trust and Collaboration

Building trust and fostering collaboration are essential components of successful leadership. This section explores how leaders can leverage insights from social neuroscience to cultivate these crucial aspects within their teams and organizations.

Understanding Trust in the Brain:

- Neurological Foundations of Trust: Trust has a tangible basis in the brain, involving structures like the amygdala and the prefrontal cortex. These areas are involved in evaluating the trustworthiness of others and making decisions based on that trust.

- Oxytocin and Trust: Research has shown that oxytocin, often referred to as the "trust hormone," plays a significant role in social bonding and trust-building. Understanding its influence can help leaders create an environment that naturally promotes trust.

Strategies for Building Trust:

- Consistency and Reliability: Consistent actions and reliability in decision-making can strengthen trust. When team members know what to expect from their leader, it creates a sense of security and reliability.

- Transparency and Open Communication: Openly sharing information, providing clear rationale for decisions, and admitting mistakes can significantly enhance trust. Transparency fosters an environment where team members feel valued and respected.

Fostering Collaboration:

- Creating a Shared Vision: Collaboration is most effective when team members are aligned towards a common goal. Leaders should work on developing and communicating a clear, compelling vision that resonates with the entire team.

- Encouraging Diverse Perspectives: A collaborative environment is one where diverse ideas and perspectives are welcomed. Leaders should encourage team members to voice their opinions and contribute their unique insights.

Overcoming Challenges in Trust and Collaboration:

- Managing Conflict: Conflict is inevitable in any team. Effective leaders use conflict as an opportunity to strengthen trust and collaboration by addressing issues openly and constructively.

- Building Trust in a Remote Environment: In remote or hybrid work settings, building trust can be more challenging. Leaders should make extra efforts to stay connected with their team, such as through regular virtual meetings and check-ins.

Real-World Examples:

- Case Studies: Illustrating successful trust and collaboration building in companies known for their strong culture, like Google or Zappos, can provide practical insights.

- Leadership Testimonials: Including testimonials from successful leaders who have effectively built trust and collaboration can offer inspiration and real-life strategies.

Real-World Example: Building Trust and Collaboration at Pixar

Background: Pixar Animation Studios, renowned for its creative and innovative culture, provides a compelling real-world example of building trust and collaboration. Under the leadership of Ed Catmull and John Lasseter, Pixar fostered an environment where trust and collaboration were central to its operations and creative processes.

Key Strategies Employed:

1. Braintrust Meetings:

   - Pixar established a unique system called the "Braintrust," which consisted of a group of experienced storytellers and filmmakers.

   - During these meetings, teams presented their work in progress and received candid feedback.

   - The key was that the feedback was not directive; the director had the freedom to use it as they saw fit. This approach built trust, as it was grounded in mutual respect and the understanding that everyone's goal was to enhance the quality of the film.

2. Emphasis on Open Communication:

   - Catmull and Lasseter encouraged open communication across all levels of the company.

   - They held regular company-wide meetings where employees could ask questions directly to the leadership, fostering transparency.

3. Physical Space Designed for Collaboration:

   - Pixar's office layout was intentionally designed to promote unplanned interactions among employees from different departments.

   - For example, having common areas like the cafeteria in the central atrium encouraged chance encounters, leading to spontaneous discussions and idea exchanges.

4. Encouraging Risk-Taking and Tolerance for Failure:

- ○ Pixar's culture embraced risk-taking and acknowledged that failure was a part of the creative process.

- ○ By creating a safe environment for taking creative risks, employees felt more comfortable sharing unconventional ideas, enhancing collaboration and innovation.

Impact:

- Enhanced Creativity and Innovation: This culture of trust and collaboration led to a string of successful movies, each breaking new ground in storytelling and animation technology.

- Employee Satisfaction and Retention: Pixar consistently ranked high in employee satisfaction, with a notable level of employee loyalty and low turnover rates.

- Industry Recognition: The studio not only achieved commercial success but also garnered critical acclaim, including multiple Academy Awards.

Conclusion: Pixar's approach to building trust and collaboration illustrates how leadership can effectively harness social dynamics to create a thriving organizational culture. By prioritizing open communication, respecting creative freedom, and designing spaces that encourage spontaneous collaboration, Pixar established a model that many other companies aspire to emulate. This example underscores the importance of leadership strategies that are deeply rooted in understanding and fostering positive social interactions within an organization.[1]

In summary, building trust and collaboration is a nuanced process that requires understanding the underlying social and neurological factors. By applying these principles, leaders can create a more cohesive, motivated, and high-performing team. This not only enhances the work environment but also contributes significantly to the overall success of the organization.

3. Leveraging Social Neuroscience for Effective Leadership

In the realm of leadership, understanding and applying principles from social neuroscience can significantly enhance a leader's effectiveness. This approach involves recognizing the impact of social dynamics on brain function and using this knowledge to foster a more cohesive, motivated, and productive team. Here's how leaders can leverage social neuroscience for effective leadership:

---

1. The example of Pixar's approach to building trust and collaboration, particularly the use of Braintrust meetings and their unique company culture, is well-documented in various business and leadership literature. A key reference for this information is: Catmull, E., & Wallace, A. (2014). *Creativity, Inc.: Overcoming the Unseen Forces That Stand in the Way of True Inspiration*. Random House. ISBN: 978-0812993011.

Understanding the Social Brain

1. Recognizing Social Needs:

   - The human brain is wired for social connection. Leaders need to understand the importance of social bonds and how feelings of inclusion or exclusion can impact employee performance and well-being.

   - For instance, the concept of 'social pain,' which is processed in the brain similarly to physical pain, highlights the importance of creating an inclusive work environment.

2. Empathy and Perspective-Taking:

   - Effective leaders use empathy to understand and resonate with their team members' emotions and perspectives.

   - Techniques like active listening and empathetic communication are crucial for leaders to connect with their team on a deeper level.

Enhancing Team Dynamics

1. Fostering Collaboration:

   - Understanding the neuroscience behind cooperation can help leaders create strategies that promote collaborative efforts.

   - This includes recognizing the role of neurotransmitters like oxytocin, which is associated with trust and bonding in social settings.

2. Conflict Resolution:

- Leaders can use insights from social neuroscience to navigate and resolve conflicts more effectively.

- This involves understanding the emotional and cognitive processes that underlie conflicts and addressing them in a way that validates all parties' perspectives.

Communication Strategies

1. Effective Messaging:

- Social neuroscience teaches us that the way a message is conveyed can significantly impact how it is received and processed.

- Leaders should focus on clear, empathetic, and engaging communication that aligns with the audience's values and concerns.

2. Non-Verbal Cues:

- Much of our social interaction is non-verbal. Leaders need to be aware of their own body language and be adept at reading others' non-verbal signals.

Implementing Change

1. Managing Resistance to Change:

- Understanding social neuroscience can help leaders manage resistance to change, a common challenge in organizations.

○ By recognizing how change can trigger threat responses in the brain, leaders can devise strategies that reduce fear and uncertainty.

2. Encouraging Adaptability:

○ Leaders can promote a culture of adaptability and learning by understanding how new experiences and challenges can foster neural growth and flexibility.

Conclusion

Leveraging social neuroscience in leadership is about understanding and applying the principles of how our brains function in social contexts. By doing so, leaders can enhance their ability to connect with, motivate, and guide their teams effectively. This approach not only improves individual and team performance but also contributes to a more positive and productive organizational culture. In an era where emotional intelligence and social skills are increasingly valued, integrating social neuroscience into leadership practices is not just beneficial but essential for long-term success.

Chapter Seven

Neuroleadership and Change Management

"The art of progress is to preserve order amid change and to preserve change amid order." – Alfred North Whitehead

1. The Brain's Resistance to Change

Understanding the brain's natural resistance to change is crucial for effective leadership and change management. This resistance is not merely a matter of stubbornness or lack of vision; it's deeply rooted in our neurobiology.

Neurological Basis for Resistance:

- The human brain is wired to favor routine and predictability. This preference is rooted in the brain's desire to conserve energy and ensure survival. The basal ganglia, a key structure in the brain, plays a significant role in habit formation and routine behaviors. When faced with change, this 'habit center' perceives it as a threat, triggering a stress response.

- The amygdala, another critical brain structure, is involved in emotional processing and fear responses. It becomes activated during periods of uncertainty and change, often leading to anxiety and resistance.

Cognitive and Emotional Aspects:

- Change challenges our existing beliefs and can create cognitive dissonance. This discomfort arises when new information conflicts with our current understanding or when we are asked to behave in ways that contradict our self-image.

- Emotionally, change can evoke feelings of fear, loss, and uncertainty. These emotions are powerful and can override logical arguments for change.

The Role of Past Experiences:

- Past experiences, stored in the hippocampus, significantly influence our response to change. Negative past experiences with change can lead to heightened resistance in future scenarios.

Implications for Leadership:

- Leaders need to recognize that resistance to change is a natural, neurologically driven response. This understanding is crucial for developing empathetic and effective strategies to manage and lead change.

- Acknowledging and addressing the emotional and psychological aspects of change can help in reducing resistance and easing the transition for employees.

Alternative Perspective: Neuroplasticity

- Norman Doidge's "The Brain That Changes Itself" presents an alternative perspective, emphasizing the brain's capacity for change and adaptation. This concept of neuroplasticity suggests that, despite a natural resistance to change, the brain can rewire itself and adapt to new circumstances.

- Understanding neuroplasticity can inspire leaders to develop strategies that leverage the brain's adaptability, facilitating smoother transitions and fostering a resilient organizational culture.

In conclusion, the brain's resistance to change is a fundamental aspect that leaders must navigate in change management. By understanding the neurological underpinnings of this resistance, leaders can develop more effective strategies that acknowledge and address these innate human responses. This approach not only facilitates smoother transitions but also fosters a more resilient and adaptable organizational culture.

2. Strategies for Leading Change Effectively

Effective change management is a critical skill for leaders, especially in the dynamic landscape of modern business. Integrating insights from neuroscience and psychology, leaders can adopt strategies that not only facilitate smoother transitions but also foster a culture embracing change as an opportunity for growth and innovation. Here are key strategies for leading change effectively:

1. Communicate Clearly and Consistently:Regular and transparent communication about the reasons for change, expected outcomes, and progress helps stabilize the emotional climate of the organization. Clear communication reduces uncertainty, a major trigger for the brain's fear response.

2. Involve Employees in the Change Process:Participation in planning and implementation can mitigate feelings of powerlessness and loss of control. This approach aligns with self-determination theory, emphasizing that autonomy is a key driver of motivation.

3. Foster a Growth Mindset:Encouraging employees to view change as an opportunity for learning and development rather than a threat can be transformative. This mindset is supported by neuroplasticity, the brain's ability to adapt and learn new things.

4. Provide Support and Training:Offering training and support during transitions builds confidence and reduces anxiety. This strategy is backed by adult learning theory, which highlights the importance of practical, hands-on experiences in adult education.

5. Recognize and Reward Adaptability:Acknowledging and rewarding efforts to embrace change reinforces adaptive behaviors. This strategy is in line with the principles of positive reinforcement, suggesting that rewarded behaviors are more likely to be repeated.

6. Lead by Example:Leaders should model the behaviors and attitudes they wish to see in their teams. This approach is consistent with social learning theory, which posits that people learn behaviors by observing and imitating others, especially those in leadership positions.

In summary, these strategies, rooted in neuroscientific and psychological insights, provide a comprehensive framework for leaders to navigate and lead change effectively. By employing these approaches, leaders can cultivate a culture that is adaptable, resilient, and forward-thinking.

3. Overcoming Resistance and Nurturing a Culture of Adaptability

Overcoming resistance to change and nurturing a culture of adaptability are essential for organizational resilience and growth. This requires a nuanced understanding of the psychological and neurological factors that drive resistance, as well as strategic approaches to foster adaptability. Here, we explore these concepts, including an in-depth example to illustrate these principles in action.

Understanding Resistance:Resistance to change often stems from fear and uncertainty. Neuroscientific research shows that change triggers the brain's threat response, leading to resistance. This is a protective mechanism, as the brain prefers predictability and routine.

Strategies to Overcome Resistance:

1. Empathy and Support: Leaders should show empathy, acknowledging the challenges and emotions employees face during change. This approach aligns with the concept of emotional intelligence in leadership.

2. Incremental Changes: Implementing change in small, manageable steps can reduce overwhelm and ease the transition process. This strategy is supported by the theory of incremental change, which suggests that small, consistent changes are more sustainable and less threatening.

3. Frequent Feedback and Communication: Keeping lines of communication open and providing regular feedback can help alleviate uncertainties and build trust.

4. Empowering Employees: Involving employees in decision-making processes can give them a sense of control and ownership over the change.

In-Depth Example: Case Study: Zappos' Holacracy TransitionZappos[1], a leading online shoe and clothing retailer, provides a notable example of managing resistance in their transition to Holacracy, a system of corporate governance with no job titles and distributed authority. This radical change faced initial resistance due to its departure from traditional hierarchical structures.

To manage this, Zappos focused on extensive employee training and open forums for discussion, allowing employees to voice concerns and ask questions. They also implemented the change in phases, starting with senior management before rolling it out company-wide. This incremental approach helped employees gradually adapt to the new system.

Despite initial challenges, this approach resulted in a more dynamic and flexible organizational structure, with increased employee engagement and collaboration. Zappos' experience highlights the importance of empathetic leadership, clear communication, and employee involvement in managing change effectively.

In conclusion, overcoming resistance and fostering a culture of adaptability involves empathetic leadership, strategic communication,

---

1. Robertson, B. J. (2015). "Holacracy: The New Management System for a Rapidly Changing World." Henry Holt and Co.

and inclusive decision-making. By understanding the neuroscientific underpinnings of resistance and employing these strategies, leaders can guide their organizations through change more effectively, as demonstrated by the Zappos case study.

Chapter Eight

Neuroleadership and Performance Optimization

"Peak performance begins with your taking complete responsibility for your life and everything that happens to you."
– Brian Tracy

1. Enhancing Brain Performance for Leadership Success

In the dynamic field of neuroleadership, enhancing brain performance is pivotal for leadership success. This comprehensive approach involves harnessing various aspects of neuroscience to improve cognitive functions, emotional intelligence, and decision-making skills, which are essential for effective leadership.

Cognitive Enhancement Strategies:

- Mindfulness and Meditation: These practices are not just for stress reduction; they also enhance cognitive abilities. Research, such as that by Jha et al. (2010), has shown that mindfulness training can bolster working memory and emotional stability, key components for effective leadership.

- Optimized Sleep Patterns: Quality sleep is crucial for cognitive functions, particularly for memory consolidation and problem-solving skills. Leaders should prioritize sleep hygiene to maintain optimal brain performance.

- Balanced Nutrition and Regular Exercise: A healthy diet and physical activity are foundational for brain health. Exercise, for instance, boosts neurogenesis and enhances cognitive functions, as evidenced by studies like those conducted by Draganski and May (2008).

- Lifelong Learning and Cognitive Challenges: Engaging in new learning experiences and intellectual challenges promotes neuroplasticity. This continuous brain development is essential for adapting to new leadership challenges.

Emotional and Social Intelligence Enhancement:

- Emotional Regulation Training: Techniques such as those derived from cognitive-behavioral therapy can help leaders manage their emotions more effectively, leading to better decision-making and interpersonal relationships.

- Social Skills Development: Understanding and improving social cognition is crucial. Leaders can benefit from training in empathy and active listening, enhancing their ability to connect with and motivate their teams.

Real-World Application and Example:

A practical application of these principles can be seen in the case of a tech company that implemented a 'Brain Health' program. This program included workshops on mindfulness, seminars on nutrition and exercise, and encouraged participation in cognitive challenges like problem-solving games and learning new languages. The result was a noticeable improvement in leadership effectiveness, decision-making, and employee engagement.

In summary, enhancing brain performance for leadership success involves a holistic approach encompassing mindfulness, sleep, nutrition, exercise, continuous learning, and emotional and social intelligence training. By integrating these strategies, leaders can significantly improve their cognitive and emotional capabilities, leading to more effective and impactful leadership.

2. Leveraging Neurofeedback and Brain-Enhancing Techniques

In the realm of neuroleadership, leveraging neurofeedback and other brain-enhancing techniques is a cutting-edge approach to optimizing leadership performance. These techniques offer leaders tools to directly influence and improve their brain function, leading to enhanced cognitive abilities, emotional regulation, and overall leadership effectiveness.

Neurofeedback:

- Definition and Mechanism: Neurofeedback is a type of biofeedback that uses real-time displays of brain activity—typically through EEG (electroencephalography)—to teach self-regulation of brain functions. By observing their brain activity, individuals can learn to control and improve their mental states.

- Application in Leadership: For leaders, neurofeedback can be particularly beneficial in enhancing focus, reducing stress, and improving emotional regulation. For instance, a leader might use neurofeedback to increase their ability to concentrate during high-stakes negotiations or to maintain calm in challenging situations.

Other Brain-Enhancing Techniques:

- Transcranial Direct Current Stimulation (tDCS): This non-invasive technique involves delivering a low electrical current to specific brain areas to enhance cognitive performance. Research has shown its potential in improving problem-solving and decision-making skills.

- Nootropics and Smart Drugs: These are substances that can improve cognitive function. While some, like caffeine, are widely used and well-understood, others require careful consideration and medical advice before use.

- Cognitive Training Programs: Software and games designed to enhance cognitive abilities, such as memory, attention, and problem-solving skills, can be useful tools for leaders. These programs are often based on principles of neuroplasticity and cognitive rehabilitation.

Real-World Example:

A notable example is a financial services firm that implemented a neurofeedback program for its executives. The program included regular sessions where leaders engaged in exercises to control and improve their focus and stress management. Over time, participants reported increased clarity in decision-making, enhanced concentration, and better emotional control during high-pressure situations.

In conclusion, leveraging neurofeedback and other brain-enhancing techniques offers leaders innovative ways to improve their brain function and leadership abilities. These methods, ranging from neurofeedback and tDCS to cognitive training programs, provide leaders with practical tools to enhance their cognitive and emotional skills, ultimately leading to more effective and impactful leadership.

3. Optimizing Brain Performance through Nutrition: The Role of Ketones and Diet in Leadership

In the pursuit of neuroleadership excellence, understanding the impact of nutrition on brain performance is crucial. Recent scientific advancements have shed light on the significant role of diet, particularly the benefits of ketones, in optimizing brain function. This subchapter explores how dietary choices can influence cognitive abilities and leadership effectiveness.

Ketones and Brain Function:

- Understanding Ketones: Ketones are alternative energy sources produced by the liver from fatty acids during periods of low food intake or carbohydrate restriction. They are known for their efficient and high-energy yield for brain cells.

- Ketones and Cognitive Performance: Research indicates that ketones can enhance cognitive functions such as clarity of thought, concentration, and memory. This is particularly relevant for leaders who require sustained mental energy and focus.

Dietary Approaches to Enhance Brain Performance:

- Ketogenic Diet: This diet involves high fat, moderate protein, and low carbohydrate intake, prompting the body to enter a state of ketosis. Leaders adopting this diet may experience improved mental clarity and energy levels.

- Mediterranean Diet: Rich in fruits, vegetables, whole grains, and healthy fats, this diet has been linked to reduced inflammation and oxidative stress, factors important for maintaining cognitive health.

- Intermittent Fasting: This eating pattern alternates between periods of eating and fasting. It has been shown to increase ketone production and may improve brain health and function.

Real-World Application:

Consider the case of a tech company CEO who adopted a ketogenic diet as part of a lifestyle change. Over several months, the CEO reported enhanced mental clarity, improved decision-making abilities, and increased stamina during long work hours. The CEO's experience mirrors findings from studies suggesting that ketone production can positively impact cognitive functions critical for leadership.

In the dynamic and demanding world of technology, leaders often face immense pressure to make rapid, yet accurate decisions, manage complex projects, and maintain high levels of energy. The story of Alex Thompson, CEO of a burgeoning tech startup, exemplifies the transformative impact of the ketogenic diet on leadership performance.

Background:

- **Initial Challenges:** Alex, a 42-year-old tech entrepreneur, found himself struggling with fluctuating energy levels and difficulty maintaining focus during long strategy meetings. Despite a healthy lifestyle, he felt his cognitive sharpness waning, impacting his decision-making and leadership effectiveness.

Adopting the Ketogenic Diet:

- **Dietary Shift:** After consulting with a nutritionist, Alex transitioned to a ketogenic diet, characterized by low carbohydrate, moderate protein, and high fat intake. This shift was aimed at enhancing his brain function through increased ketone production.

- **Gradual Adaptation:** The initial phase involved overcoming the 'keto flu,' a temporary state as his body adjusted to burning fat for fuel instead of carbohydrates. Alex experienced fatigue and brain fog, which subsided after a few weeks.

Outcomes:

- **Enhanced Cognitive Performance:** Within two months, Alex reported significant improvements in mental clarity and focus. He attributed this to the steady energy supply from ketones, unlike the fluctuations experienced with glucose.

- **Improved Decision-Making:** With heightened clarity, Alex found himself making quicker and more confident decisions, a crucial aspect of leading a fast-paced tech company.

- **Increased Stamina:** Long hours and back-to-back meetings became more manageable. Alex noted a substantial increase in his stamina and overall energy levels.

Scientific Correlation:

- **Research Support:** Alex's experience aligns with studies indicating that ketones can provide a more efficient and sustained energy source for the brain, enhancing cognitive functions. For instance, a study by Krikorian et al. (2012) demonstrated improved memory and cognitive function in older adults following a ketogenic intervention.

- **Broader Implications:** This case highlights the potential of dietary interventions, like the ketogenic diet, in boosting the cognitive capabilities of leaders in high-pressure environments.

Alex Thompson's journey with the ketogenic diet underscores the profound impact that nutritional choices can have on leadership performance. By harnessing the power of ketones, leaders like Alex can enhance their cognitive functions, decision-making abilities, and overall endurance, essential for navigating the challenges of the modern business world.

In summary, optimizing brain performance through nutrition, particularly the role of ketones and diet, is a vital aspect of neuroleadership. By understanding and implementing dietary strategies such as the ketogenic and Mediterranean diets, and intermittent fasting, leaders can enhance their cognitive functions and overall leadership effectiveness. This approach not only contributes to personal health and well-being but also sets a positive example for creating a high-performing culture within organizations.

Chapter Nine

Neuroleadership and Ethical Decision Making

"**E**thics is knowing the difference between what you have a right to do and what is right to do." – Potter Stewart

1. The Neuroscience of Ethics and Morality

Understanding the neuroscience of ethics and morality is pivotal for leaders who aim to foster ethical decision-making within their organizations. This exploration delves into how brain mechanisms underpin our moral judgments and ethical behaviors, offering insights crucial for effective leadership.

Neurological Foundations of Moral Reasoning:

1. Prefrontal Cortex: The prefrontal cortex plays a crucial role in moral reasoning and ethical decision-making. It is involved in complex cognitive processes such as evaluating consequences, understanding social norms, and empathizing with others.

2. Amygdala: The amygdala, associated with emotional processing, is integral to our moral responses, particularly those involving empathy and fear. It helps in assessing the emotional aspects of moral situations.

3. Mirror Neurons: These neurons, found in various brain regions, are thought to be involved in understanding others' intentions and emotions, a key aspect of empathy and moral cognition.

Moral Intuition vs. Moral Reasoning:

Recent studies suggest that moral decision-making often involves a blend of intuitive and reasoned processes. The brain's automatic, emotional responses (largely mediated by the amygdala) often guide initial moral intuitions, which are then refined by more deliberate, cognitive processes (mediated by the prefrontal cortex).

Implications for Leadership:

Understanding these neural mechanisms can help leaders appreciate the complexity of ethical decision-making. It underscores the importance of creating environments that encourage both intuitive and reflective moral reasoning, ensuring that decisions are not solely based on immediate emotional responses but are also thoughtfully considered.

Conclusion:

The neuroscience of ethics and morality provides a deeper understanding of how leaders can cultivate ethical decision-making within their organizations. By acknowledging the intricate interplay between different brain regions and processes, leaders can develop strategies that promote a balanced approach to ethics, combining intuitive moral sensibilities with rational deliberation.

2. Ethical Leadership in the Business Context

Ethical leadership in the business world is not just about adhering to legal standards and company policies; it's about creating a culture of integrity and accountability. This section explores the role of ethical leadership in shaping organizational culture and influencing business practices.

Defining Ethical Leadership:

Ethical leadership involves demonstrating behaviors that are in line with ethical principles and values, and influencing others to do the same. It encompasses aspects like honesty, fairness, and social responsibility. Ethical leaders are role models, setting standards for what is acceptable and expected in the organization.

Impact on Organizational Culture:

1. **Trust Building:** Ethical leadership fosters trust among employees, stakeholders, and customers. When leaders consistently act ethically, they build a reputation for reliability and integrity, which is crucial for long-term success.

2. **Employee Morale and Engagement:** Organizations led by ethical leaders often report higher levels of employee satisfaction and engagement. Employees are more likely to be committed and motivated when they feel they are part of an ethical and just environment.

3. **Risk Mitigation:** Ethical leadership helps in identifying and mitigating risks associated with unethical behavior, such as legal penalties, reputational damage, and financial losses.

Challenges in Ethical Leadership:

Navigating ethical dilemmas in business can be complex. Leaders often face situations where the right course of action is not clear-cut, requiring a balance between different stakeholders' interests and ethical considerations.

Strategies for Promoting Ethical Leadership:

1. **Clear Ethical Standards:** Establishing and communicating clear ethical guidelines is essential. This includes having a well-defined code of conduct and ensuring that it is integrated into all aspects of the business.

2. **Training and Development:** Regular training on ethical issues helps employees recognize and deal with ethical dilemmas. Leadership development programs should also emphasize ethical decision-making skills.

3. **Ethical Decision-Making Frameworks:** Implementing decision-making frameworks that incorporate ethical considerations can guide leaders in making choices that align with the organization's values.

4. **Encouraging Whistleblowing:** Creating a safe and anonymous way for employees to report unethical behavior is crucial for maintaining ethical standards.

Conclusion:

Ethical leadership is a cornerstone of sustainable business success. By embedding ethical values into the fabric of the organization, leaders can create a positive and principled business environment. This not only enhances the company's reputation but also contributes to a more equitable and responsible business landscape.

3. Applying Neuroethical Principles to Business Practices

Incorporating neuroethical principles into business practices involves understanding and applying the insights gained from neuroscience to ensure ethical decision-making and behavior within organizations. This section explores how neuroethical principles can be integrated into business practices and provides a real-life example to illustrate their application.

Understanding Neuroethics in Business:

Neuroethics, a field at the intersection of neuroscience and ethics, examines the implications of our growing understanding of the brain on ethical behavior. In the business context, this involves considering how brain-based insights can influence ethical decision-making and organizational conduct.

Key Areas of Application:

1. **Decision-Making:** Understanding the neural basis of decision-making can help in creating frameworks that promote

ethical choices. This includes recognizing and mitigating biases and ensuring decisions align with both organizational values and societal norms.

2. **Leadership Development:** Training programs for leaders can incorporate neuroethical principles, emphasizing the importance of ethical decision-making and the impact of leadership behavior on employee well-being and moral conduct.

3. **Organizational Policies:** Developing policies that reflect an understanding of ethical behavior from a neurological perspective. This could involve policies related to diversity and inclusion, mental health, and employee engagement.

Strategies for Implementation:

1. **Ethical Training and Awareness:** Conducting regular training sessions that focus on neuroethics, helping employees understand the brain processes behind ethical dilemmas and decision-making.

2. **Behavioral Guidelines:** Establishing clear behavioral guidelines that reflect neuroethical principles, ensuring that all employees understand the expected ethical standards.

3. **Encouraging Open Dialogue:** Creating an environment where ethical issues can be discussed openly, encouraging employees to share their views and concerns.

Real-World Example:

Example: A Multinational Corporation's Ethical Transformation[1]

A multinational corporation, facing criticism for unethical business practices, embarked on a journey to overhaul its ethical standards. The company integrated neuroethical principles into its core business strategies, focusing on transparent and ethical decision-making processes.

1. **Leadership Workshops:** The company conducted workshops for its leaders, emphasizing the importance of ethical behavior and decision-making based on neuroscientific insights.

2. **Policy Overhaul:** The organization revised its policies, incorporating neuroethical considerations, particularly in areas like marketing practices and employee well-being.

3. **Ethics Committees:** The company established ethics committees responsible for monitoring and guiding ethical practices across different departments.

4. **Outcome:** This transformation led to a significant improvement in the company's reputation, employee morale, and customer trust. The company's commitment to neuroethical principles was recognized in various industry forums, setting a new standard for ethical conduct in its sector.

---

1. Schermer, M., & Pinch, T. (2015). Ethical issues in neuromarketing: "I consume, therefore I am!" *Science and Engineering Ethics*, 21(5), 1271-1284.

Conclusion:

Applying neuroethical principles to business practices is not only about compliance with ethical standards but also about creating a culture that values ethical behavior at its core. By understanding and applying insights from neuroscience, businesses can foster an environment of ethical decision-making, enhancing their reputation and contributing positively to society.

Chapter Ten

Practical Applications of Neuroleadership

"Great things are done by a series of small things brought together." – Vincent Van Gogh

1. Neuroleadershipin Hiring and Talent Management

The application of neuroleadership principles in hiring and talent management represents a significant shift in how organizations approach these crucial aspects of business. By leveraging insights from neuroscience, companies can refine their hiring processes, enhance talent management strategies, and ultimately build a workforce that is not only skilled but also neurologically diverse and adaptable.

Innovative Hiring Practices:

1. Neuroscience-Informed Job Interviews: Traditional interviews often fail to assess a candidate's true potential. Incorporating neuroscience principles, such as understanding emotional intelligence and cognitive abilities, can lead to more effective evaluation methods. For instance, behavioral questions that assess a candidate's response to real-world scenarios can provide insights into their problem-solving and emotional regulation skills.

2. Biometric Assessments: Some organizations are exploring biometric tools that measure physiological responses, such as heart rate variability, to assess a candidate's stress resilience and emotional regulation capabilities. These tools, used ethically and with consent, can complement traditional assessment methods.

Enhancing Talent Management:

1. Personalized Development Plans: Understanding that each brain is unique, neuroleadership advocates for personalized development plans. These plans can be tailored based on an individual's neurological strengths and areas for growth, identified through assessments and continuous feedback.

2. Neuroplasticity-Driven Training: Emphasizing the brain's ability to learn and adapt, training programs can be designed to encourage neuroplasticity. This involves creating challenging, diverse, and engaging learning experiences that stimulate the brain and foster skill development.

3. Mental Health and Well-being: Recognizing the impact of

mental health on performance, neuroleadership encourages organizations to prioritize employee well-being. This can include initiatives like mindfulness training, stress management workshops, and creating a supportive work environment.

Real-World Application:

Example: A Technology Firm's Neuro-Inclusive Hiring Strategy[1]

A leading technology firm revamped its hiring process to incorporate neuroleadership principles, focusing on attracting neurodiverse talent. The firm recognized that individuals with different neurological profiles, such as those on the autism spectrum, can bring unique skills and perspectives.

1. Customized Interview Processes: The firm developed alternative interview methods for neurodiverse candidates, such as work trials or practical assessments, instead of traditional interviews that could be challenging for some candidates.

2. Neurodiversity Training for Hiring Managers: Hiring managers received training on neurodiversity, helping them understand and appreciate the different ways candidates might process information and communicate.

3. Outcome: This approach not only broadened the firm's talent pool but also enhanced its innovation capacity. The neurodiverse hires brought unique problem-solving skills and attention to detail, contributing significantly to various projects.

---

1. Austin, R. D., & Pisano, G. P. (2017). Neurodiversity as a Competitive Advantage. *Harvard Business Review*.

Conclusion:

Neuroleadership in hiring and talent management is about moving beyond conventional practices and embracing a more inclusive, brain-based approach. By understanding and valuing neurological diversity, organizations can create a more dynamic, innovative, and resilient workforce.

2. Neuroleadership in Team Building and Collaboration

Neuroleadership offers a unique perspective on team building and collaboration, emphasizing the neurological underpinnings of social interaction, communication, and group dynamics. By applying neuroscientific insights, leaders can foster more cohesive, innovative, and effective teams.

Enhancing Team Dynamics:

1. **Understanding Social Brain Networks:** Recognizing the role of social brain networks, such as the mirror neuron system and the theory of mind network, can help leaders facilitate better communication and empathy within teams. This understanding can lead to more effective conflict resolution and a stronger sense of team cohesion.

2. **Diversity and Neurological Inclusivity:** Embracing neurological diversity in teams can enhance creativity and problem-solving. Leaders can create teams with a mix of neurologically diverse individuals, ensuring a balance of analytical and creative thinkers, detail-oriented and big-picture processors.

Promoting Collaborative Environments:

1. **Psychological Safety:** Creating an environment where team members feel safe to express ideas and take risks is crucial. Leaders can foster psychological safety by encouraging open communication, showing vulnerability, and appreciating diverse viewpoints.

2. **Rewarding Collaborative Behaviors:** Implementing reward systems that recognize and incentivize teamwork and collaboration can reinforce these behaviors. This could include team-based achievements in performance evaluations and recognition programs.

Leveraging Technology for Collaboration:

1. **Digital Collaboration Tools:** Utilizing digital tools that facilitate collaboration, especially in remote or hybrid work environments, can enhance team dynamics. These tools can range from project management software to virtual reality environments for brainstorming sessions.

2. **Data-Driven Insights:** Using data analytics to understand team dynamics and performance can provide leaders with objective insights to make informed decisions about team composition and collaboration strategies.

Real-World Application:

Example: A Global Consulting Firm's Collaborative Culture Shift[2]

A global consulting firm implemented a neuroleadership-driven approach to enhance team collaboration and effectiveness. Recognizing the importance of social connections and psychological safety, the firm undertook several initiatives:

1. **Team Building Workshops:** The firm organized workshops focused on understanding brain-based differences in communication and problem-solving styles, helping team members appreciate and leverage their diverse strengths.

2. **Collaboration-Focused Performance Metrics:** The firm revised its performance evaluation criteria to include metrics related to teamwork and collaboration, encouraging employees to work together more effectively.

3. **Outcome:** These initiatives led to a noticeable improvement in team performance and employee satisfaction. Teams became more adept at navigating complex projects, and there was a significant increase in innovative solutions developed by these teams.

Conclusion:

Neuroleadership's application in team building and collaboration is about understanding and leveraging the brain's social nature. By

2. Edmondson, A. (2019). The Fearless Organization: Creating Psychological Safety in the Workplace for Learning, Innovation, and Growth. Wiley

creating environments that respect neurological diversity and promote psychological safety, leaders can cultivate teams that are not only high-performing but also resilient and adaptable to change.

Chapter Eleven

The SCARF Model - A Neuroleadership Perspective

"In the realm of leadership, understanding the brain is not just about neuroscience; it's about insight into the human condition. The SCARF Model reminds us that every interaction in leadership is a chance to either activate threat or reward in the minds of those we lead." – Thomas Allan

Introduction to the SCARF Model[1]:

The SCARF model, developed by Dr. David Rock in 2008, is a cornerstone concept in neuroleadership. It provides a framework for understanding key social triggers that can either enhance or diminish our brain's engagement in social interactions. SCARF stands for Status, Certainty, Autonomy, Relatedness, and Fairness. This model is particularly relevant for leaders seeking to create positive, productive work environments.

1. Status: The Need for Recognition and Respect

Status refers to our perception of our importance relative to others. In a leadership context, recognizing and valuing the contributions of team members can significantly boost their motivation and engagement. Leaders can enhance the status of their team members by providing positive feedback, public recognition, and opportunities for professional growth.

Real-World Application: A technology firm introduced a peer-recognition program, leading to a notable increase in employee satisfaction and a decrease in turnover. Employees were encouraged to publicly acknowledge their colleagues' achievements, which significantly enhanced the sense of status among team members.

2. Certainty: Craving Predictability and Clarity

The human brain is wired to seek certainty to minimize threats and reduce stress. Leaders can address this need by communicating

---

1. Rock, D. (2008). SCARF: A Brain-Based Model for Collaborating With and Influencing Others. NeuroLeadership Journal.

clearly, setting well-defined goals, and providing regular updates on organizational changes or decisions.

Real-World Application: During a major restructuring, a multinational corporation implemented transparent communication strategies. Regular updates and clear explanations of changes provided employees with a sense of certainty, resulting in improved morale and productivity.

3. Autonomy: The Power of Empowerment

Autonomy is about having a sense of control over our work and environment. Leaders can foster autonomy by delegating responsibilities, encouraging independent decision-making, and allowing flexibility in how tasks are accomplished.

Real-World Application: A startup adopted a flat organizational structure, granting employees significant decision-making autonomy. This empowerment led to innovative solutions and rapid growth, as employees felt more in control and invested in the company's success.

4. Relatedness: Building Trust and Connection

Relatedness involves feeling safe and connected with others. Leaders can strengthen relatedness by creating a team culture that values collaboration, inclusivity, and mutual support.

Real-World Application: A case study of a healthcare organization that enhanced team performance and patient care by focusing on team-building activities and collaborative projects.

5. Fairness: The Importance of Equity and Transparency

Fairness is about being treated justly and impartially. Leaders can promote fairness by ensuring transparent decision-making processes, equitable resource distribution, and unbiased treatment of all team members.

Real-World Application: A major retail company overhauled its corporate policies to address fairness in pay and promotion. This move improved employee trust and loyalty, as the workforce perceived the company's efforts to ensure equitable treatment and transparency.

Conclusion: Integrating SCARF into Leadership Practice

Understanding and applying the SCARF model can significantly enhance a leader's ability to engage and motivate their team. By addressing these five social domains, leaders can create a work environment that supports the psychological needs of their employees, leading to higher levels of satisfaction, productivity, and overall organizational success.

The SCARF model provides a practical and neuroscience-based approach to enhancing leadership effectiveness. By understanding and addressing the fundamental social needs of status, certainty, autonomy, relatedness, and fairness, leaders can cultivate a more engaged, motivated, and high-performing team.

Conclusion

The Journey of Neuroleadership - Past, Present, and Future

"Neuroleadership is the convergence of art and science, where the mysteries of the brain meet the complexity of human behavior, creating leaders who are not only effective but also compassionate and wise." - Thomas Allan

As we reach the conclusion of this exploration into neuroleadership, it's essential to reflect on the journey we've undertaken, the current landscape, and the exciting possibilities that lie ahead.

Where We've Been:

Neuroleadership has evolved from a nascent idea into a robust field of study and practice. Initially, leadership was viewed through the lens of inherent traits and behaviors. However, as our understanding of the brain deepened, so did our insights into leadership. The integration of neuroscience into leadership studies has revolutionized how we perceive and develop leadership skills.

Where We Are Today:

Currently, neuroleadership stands at a pivotal point. It has provided us with profound insights into decision-making, emotional intelligence, motivation, and team dynamics. Leaders today are equipped with tools and strategies grounded in neuroscience, enabling them to enhance their effectiveness and foster high-performing, adaptable organizations.

Where We Are Going:

Looking ahead, the next decade promises even greater integration of neuroscientific insights into leadership. Advancements in brain imaging and cognitive neuroscience will offer deeper understandings of how we can optimize brain function for leadership. We may see personalized leadership development plans based on individual neurological profiles and even more sophisticated neurofeedback tools for performance enhancement.

What You Can Do Now:

To start incorporating the principles of neuroleadership into your daily life, begin with self-awareness. Reflect on your decision-making processes, emotional responses, and interactions with others. Seek feedback and be open to learning and adapting. Embrace a growth mindset, recognizing that your brain's capacity to change and adapt is one of your greatest assets as a leader.

Incorporating Neuroleadership Principles:

1. **Practice Mindfulness:** Regular mindfulness practices can enhance focus, emotional regulation, and stress management.

2. **Engage in Lifelong Learning:** Continuously challenge your brain with new information and experiences to foster neuroplasticity.

3. **Foster Inclusive Leadership:** Understand and appreciate the neurological diversity within your teams to create more innovative and resilient organizations.

Final Thoughts:

As we embark on the future of neuroleadership, remember that the journey is as important as the destination. The field is ever-evolving, and as leaders, our learning never stops. Embrace the principles of neuroleadership, and you will not only transform your leadership but also contribute to a future where leadership is more humane, effective, and aligned with the intricate workings of the human brain.

This book is a journey through the landscape of neuroleadership, offering insights and strategies to enhance your leadership capabilities. As you apply these principles, you are not only advancing your career but also contributing to a more empathetic, effective, and neurologically informed world of leadership.

Afterword

Your input and feedback through reviews are tremendously important. They guide others in their decision to explore this book. If you've found fresh insights, been led to reconsider your perspectives, discovered practical actions for change, or affirmed your current effective practices, we invite you to share your experiences in a review. Your endorsement would mean the world to us, so if you can spare 5 minutes, I would truly appreciate it. I can't thank you enough for your support and your role in this book's success - you make a big difference!

Finally, I am grateful for your commitment, both in reading this book and sharing your thoughts. Your involvement is priceless in ensuring the sustained growth of the Magnetic Mindset Leadership. We're excited to hear from you!

With gratitude,

Thomas Allan

Also By Thomas Allan

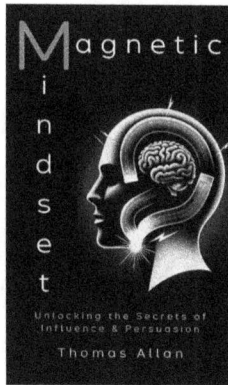

The Magnetic Mindset:
Unlocking the Secrets of Influence and Persuasion

Whether you're in a leadership role, looking to ascend the career ladder, or simply desire to have a stronger influence on those around you, this book is your golden ticket.

Featured as **#1 Amazon Hot New Release** in Sales &
Selling Management.
Learn from an expert how to go beyond mere selling to
genuinely connect with people.
Discover the **blend of psychology, communication, and
real-life application** that makes the Magnetic Mindset
unique.

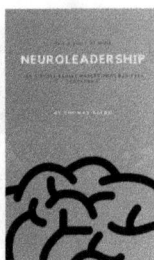

Neuroleadership: The Science Behind Exceptional Business Leadership

Effective leadership isn't just about strategic decisions
and management skills; **it's about truly understanding
the intricacies of the human brain.**

PROFIT HACKING

THOMAS ALLAN

Profit Hacking: Strategies for Explosive Profit Growth in the Modern Business Business World

This book isn't just theory; it's a collection of battle-tested strategies and tools frequently compared to the insights in top entrepreneur books. What sets it apart is its no-nonsense, actionable approach that empowers you to implement effective Lead-to-Revenue Management (L2RM) strategies from Day 1.

BRANDING BRILLIANCE

THOMAS ALLAN

Branding Brilliance: Your Blueprint to Creating & Communicating an Irresistible Personal Brand

In today's digital world, personal branding is no longer optional. We all have a personal brand, whether or not we are aware of it. It's how the world sees us and can significantly impact our careers and lives. This **workbook** is designed to guide you through the process of creating a personal brand that truly reflects who you are and what you stand for.

a

https://magnet-mind.com/book

in

https://magnet-mind.com/linkedin

About Author

Thomas Allan

As an executive coach, he relishes the opportunity to inspire leaders around the world, urging them to adopt a growth mindset and enhance their leadership prowess. He holds a special place in his heart for small business owners, helping them decipher the recipe for success in today's business climate.

He shares his insights into mindset development, leadership, and profit optimization on his blog at magneticmindsetblog.com and is the author of the following publications:

· **Profit Hacking:** *Unlocking Revenue, Maximizing Profit. Get the lead and Keep the Lead. Strategies for explosive profit growth in the modern business world.*

· **Branding Brilliance:** *Your Blueprint to Creating and Communicating an Irresistible Personal Brand.*

· **Magnetic Mindset:** *Unlocking the Secrets of Influence & Persuasion*

Through his weekly blog, available at https://magneticmindsetblog.com, Thomas continues to influence a growing audience with insights into mindset development, leadership, and profit optimization.

Scan the QR Code to Link to Blog

Thomas Allan is a multifaceted professional who combines his wide-ranging experience and knowledge to inspire and empower individuals and organizations. His influence extends beyond his writings, reaching those he coaches and consults to succeed personally and professionally, significantly impacting today's fast-paced business landscape.

References

Allan, T. (2023). The Magnetic Mindset: Unlocking the Secrets of Influence and Persuasion. Available at: https://www.amazon.com/dp/B0C3L2BMXK

Arnsten, A. F. T. (2009). Stress signalling pathways that impair prefrontal cortex structure and function. Nature Reviews Neuroscience, 10(6), 410-422.

Austin, R. D., & Pisano, G. P. (2017). Neurodiversity as a Competitive Advantage. Harvard Business Review.

Bandura, A. (1977). "Social Learning Theory." General Learning Press. Bandura, A. (1977). "Social Learning Theory." General Learning Press.

Batson, C. D. (2009). These Things Called Empathy: Eight Related but Distinct Phenomena. In J. Decety & W. Ickes (Eds.), The Social Neuroscience of Empathy (pp. 3-15). MIT Press.

Bechara, A., Damasio, H., Tranel, D., & Damasio, A. R. (2005). The Iowa Gambling Task and the somatic marker hypothesis: some questions and answers. Trends in Cognitive Sciences, 9(4), 159-162.

Bush, G., Luu, P., & Posner, M. I. (2000). Cognitive and emotional influences in anterior cingulate cortex. Trends in Cognitive Sciences, 4(6), 215-222.

Carlyle, T. (1841). On Heroes, Hero-Worship, and The Heroic in History. James Fraser.

Catmull, E., & Wallace, A. (2014). Creativity, Inc.: Overcoming the Unseen Forces That Stand in the Way of True Inspiration. Random House. ISBN: 978-0812993011.

Damasio, A. R. (1994). Descartes' Error: Emotion, Reason, and the Human Brain. Putnam.

Decety, J., & Cacioppo, S. (2012). The speed of morality: A high-density electrical neuroimaging study. Journal of Neurophysiology, 108(11), 3068-3072.

Deci, E. L., & Ryan, R. M. (2000). "The 'What' and 'Why' of Goal Pursuits: Human Needs and the Self-Determination of Behavior." Psychological Inquiry.

Diamond, A. (2013). Executive Functions. Annual Rview of Psychology, 64, 135-168.

Doidge, N. (2007). "The Brain That Changes Itself: Stories of Personal Triumph from the Frontiers of Brain Science." Viking.

Draganski, B., & May, A. (2008). Training-induced structural changes in the adult human brain. Behavioural Brain Research, 192(1), 137-142.

Dweck, C. S. (2006). "Mindset: The New Psychology of Success." Random House.

Edmondson, A. (2019). The Fearless Organization: Creating Psychological Safety in the Workplace for Learning, Innovation, and Growth. Wiley.

Eichenbaum, H. (2000). A cortical-hippocampal system for declarative memory. Nature Reviews Neuroscience, 1(1), 41-50.

Ericsson, K. A., & Pool, R. (2016). Peak: Secrets from the New Science of Expertise. Houghton Mifflin Harcourt.

Fiedler, F. E. (1967). A theory of leadership effectiveness. McGraw-Hill.

Frith, C. D., & Frith, U. (2006). The neural basis of mentalizing. Neuron, 50(4), 531-534.

George, J. M. (2000). Emotions and Leadership: The Role of Emotional Intelligence. Human Relations, 53(8), 1027-1055.

Goleman, D. (2005). Emotional Intelligence. Bantam Books.

Goleman, D., Boyatzis, R., & McKee, A. (2002). Primal Leadership: Learning to Lead with Emotional Intelligence. Harvard Business School Press.

Graybiel, A. M. (2008). Habits, rituals, and the evaluative brain. Annual Review of Neuroscience, 31, 359-387.

Greene, J. D., Nystrom, L. E., Engell, A. D., Darley, J. M., & Cohen, J. D. (2004). The neural bases of cognitive conflict and control in moral judgment. Neuron, 44(2), 389-400.

Gruzelier, J. H. (2014). EEG-neurofeedback for optimising performance. I: A review of cognitive and affective outcome in healthy participants. Neuroscience & Biobehavioral Reviews, 44, 124-141.

Haidt, J. (2001). The emotional dog and its rational tail: A social intuitionist approach to moral judgment. Psychological Review, 108(4), 814.

Hatfield, E., Cacioppo, J. T., & Rapson, R. L. (1994). Emotional Contagion. Cambridge University Press.

Heath, C., & Heath, D. (2007). "Made to Stick: Why Some Ideas Survive and Others Die." Random House. This book emphasizes the importance of clear and compelling communication in making ideas stick, a principle crucial in change management.

Heath, C., & Heath, D. (2007). "Made to Stick: Why Some Ideas Survive and Others Die." Random House.

Hillman, C. H., Erickson, K. I., & Kramer, A. F. (2008). Be smart, exercise your heart: exercise effects on brain and cognition. Nature Reviews Neuroscience, 9(1), 58-65.

Jha, A. P., Stanley, E. A., Kiyonaga, A., Wong, L., & Gelfand, L. (2010). Examining the protective effects of mindfulness training on working memory capacity and affective experience. Emotion, 10(1), 54-64.

Kabat-Zinn, J. (1994). Wherever You Go, There You Are: Mindfulness Meditation in Everyday Life. Hyperion.

Kable, J. W., & Glimcher, P. W. (2009). The neurobiology of decision: consensus and controversy. Neuron, 63(6), 733-745.

Kadosh, R. C., Levy, N., O'Shea, J., Shea, N., & Savulescu, J. (2012). The neuroethics of non-invasive brain stimulation. Current Biology, 22(4), R108-R111.

Kahneman, D. (2011). Thinking, Fast and Slow. Farrar, Straus and Giroux.

Kahneman, D., Slovic, P., & Tversky, A. (1982). Judgment under Uncertainty: Heuristics and Biases. Cambridge University Press.

Knowles, M. S., Holton III, E. F., & Swanson, R. A. (2005). "The Adult Learner." Elsevier.

Kotter, J. P. (1996). Leading Change. Harvard Business School Press.

Krikorian, R., Shidler, M. D., Dangelo, K., Couch, S. C., Benoit, S. C., & Clegg, D. J. (2012). Dietary ketosis enhances memory in mild cognitive impairment. Neurobiology of Aging, 33(2), 425.e19-425.e27.

LeDoux, J. E. (2000). Emotion circuits in the brain. Annual Review of Neuroscience, 23(1), 155-184.

Lewin, K., Lippitt, R., & White, R. K. (1939). Patterns of aggressive behavior in experimentally created social climates. Journal of Social Psychology, 10(2), 271-299.

Lopes, P. N., Grewal, D., Kadis, J., Gall, M., & Salovey, P. (2006). Evidence that Emotional Intelligence is Related to Job Performance and Affect and Attitudes at Work. Psicothema, 18, 132-138.

Mayer, J. D., & Salovey, P. (1997). What is emotional intelligence? In P. Salovey & D. J. Sluyter (Eds.), Emotional Development and Emotional Intelligence: Educational Implications (pp. 3-31). Basic Books.

McEwen, B. S. (2007). Physiology and Neurobiology of Stress and Adaptation: Central Role of the Brain. Physiological Reviews, 87(3), 873-904.

Miller, E. K., & Cohen, J. D. (2001). An integrative theory of prefrontal cortex function. Annual Review of Neuroscience, 24, 167-202.

Murray, A. J., Knight, N. S., Cole, M. A., Cochlin, L. E., Carter, E., Tchabanenko, K., ... & Clarke, K. (2016). Novel ketone diet enhances physical and cognitive performance. FASEB Journal, 30(12), 4021-4032.

Ochsner, K. N., & Gross, J. J. (2005). The cognitive control of emotion. Trends in Cognitive Sciences, 9(5), 242-249.

Peters, J., & Büchel, C. (2010). Neural representations of subjective reward value. Behavioural Brain Research, 213(2), 135-141.

Phelps, E. A., Lempert, K. M., & Sokol-Hessner, P. (2014). Emotion and decision making: multiple modulatory neural circuits. Annual Review of Neuroscience, 37, 263-287.

Pink, D. H. (2009). Drive: The Surprising Truth About What Motivates Us. Riverhead Books.

Ringleb, A. H., & Rock, D. (2008). NeuroLeadership: A journey through the brain for business leaders. NeuroLeadership Institute.

Rizzolatti, G., & Craighero, L. (2004). The mirror-neuron system. Annual Review of Neuroscience, 27, 169-192.

Robertson, B. J. (2015). "Holacracy: The New Management System for a Rapidly Changing World." Henry Holt and Co.

Rock D. (2009). Your Brain at Work. HarperCollins.

Rock, D. (2008). SCARF: A brain-based model for collaborating with and influencing others. NeuroLeadership Journal, 1.

Rock, D., & Schwartz, J. (2006). The neuroscience of leadership. Harvard Business Review.

Schermer, M., & Pinch, T. (2015). Ethical issues in neuromarketing: "I consume, therefore I am!" Science and Engineering Ethics 21(5), 1271-1284.

Schultz, W. (2007). Behavioral dopamine signals. Trends in Neurosciences, 30(5), 203-210.

Skinner, B. F. (1953). "Science and Human Behavior." Free Press.

Sofi, F., Cesari, F., Abbate, R., Gensini, G. F., & Casini, A. (2008). Adherence to Mediterranean diet and health status: meta-analysis. BMJ, 337, a1344.

Treviño, L. K., Hartman, L. P., & Brown, M. (2000). Moral person and moral manager: How executives develop a reputation for ethical leadership. California Management Review, 42(4), 128-142.

Ury, W. (1991). Getting Past No: Negotiating in Difficult Situations. Bantam Books.

Valentine, S., & Fleischman, G. (2008). Ethics programs, perceived corporate social responsibility and job satisfaction. Journal of Business Ethics, 77(2), 159-172.